Overcoming Childhood Trauma

The aim of the **Overcoming** series is to enable people with psychologically based disorders to take control of their own recovery program. Each title, with its specially tailored program, is devised by a practising clinician using the latest techniques of cognitive behavioral therapy – techniques which have been shown to be highly effective in changing the way patients think about themselves and their problems.

The series was initiated in 1993 by Peter Cooper, Professor of Psychology at Reading University and Research Fellow at the University of Cambridge, whose original volume on overcoming bulimia nervosa and binge-eating continues to help many people in the USA, the UK and Europe.

OVERCOMING CHILDHOOD TRAUMA

A *self-help guide using cognitive behavioral techniques*

Helen Kennerley

NEW YORK UNIVERSITY PRESS
Washington Square, New York

First published in the U.S.A. by
New York University Press
Washington Square,
New York, NY 10003

CIP data available from the Library of Congress

ISBN 0-8147-4753-1

Important Note
This book is not intended to be a substitute for any medical advice or
treatment. Any person with a condition requiring medical attention
should consult a qualified medical practitioner or suitable therapist.

Printed and bound in the EU

Contents

Contents

Acknowledgments

The recovery program outlined in this book is based on the ideas of Aaron T. Beck but, over the last ten years or so, the comments of colleagues and clients have helped to reshape the program so that it better meets the needs of survivors of childhood trauma. I am grateful to each for their feedback.

I feel that the comments from clients have been most valuable. Without them, the program might well have been no more than a theory-based protocol, rather than an approach that is really meaningful for the reader.

Professionally, my colleagues Rachel Norris, Gillian Butler, Linette Whitehead and Joan Kirk have also contributed to the "fine tuning" of the ideas in this book, and Claire Middle helped in proof-reading.

At home, Udo Kischka generously read through drafts of the book and, I think, helped make the text much more user-friendly.

Many "case examples" are used in this book in order to make the text more accessible. Although all of the descriptions are based on my clinical experiences, none of them reflects an actual person, with the exception of "Lucy." Rather, descriptions are compilations of real experiences which are used to illustrate a point.

Introduction

Why Cognitive Behavior Therapy?

Over the past two or three decades, there has been something of a revolution in the field of psychological treatment. Freud and his followers had a major impact on the way in which psychological therapy was conceptualized, and psychoanalysis and psychodynamic psychotherapy dominated the field for the first half of this century. So, long-term treatments were offered which were designed to uncover the childhood roots of personal problems – offered, that is, to those who could afford it. There was some attempt by a few health service practitioners with a public conscience to modify this form of treatment (by, for example, offering short-term treatment or group therapy), but the demand for help was so great that this had little impact. Also, whilst numerous case histories can be found of people who are convinced that psychotherapy did help them, practitioners of this form of therapy showed remarkably little interest in demonstrating that what they were offering their patients was, in fact, helpful.

As a reaction to the exclusivity of psychodynamic therapies and the slender evidence for their usefulness, in the 1950s and 1960s a set of techniques was developed, broadly collectively termed "behavior therapy". These techniques shared two basic features. First, they aimed to remove symptoms (such as anxiety) by dealing with those symptoms themselves, rather than their deep-seated underlying historical causes. Secondly, they were techniques, loosely related to what laboratory psychologists were finding out about the mechanisms of learning, which were formulated in testable terms. Indeed, practitioners of behavior therapy were committed to using techniques of proven value or, at worst, of a form which could potentially be put to the test. The area where these techniques proved of most value was in the treatment of anxiety disorders, especially specific phobias (such as fear of animals or of heights) and agoraphobia, both notoriously difficult to treat using conventional psychotherapies.

After an initial flush of enthusiasm, discontent with behavior therapy grew. There were a number of reasons for this, an important one of which was the fact that behavior therapy did not deal with the internal thoughts which were so obviously central to the distress that patients were experiencing. In this context, the fact that behavior therapy proved so inadequate when it came to the treatment of depression highlighted the need for major revision. In the late 1960s and early 1970s a treatment was developed specifically for depression called "cognitive therapy". The pioneer in this enterprise was an American psychiatrist, Professor Aaron T. Beck, who developed a theory of depression which emphasized the importance of people's depressed styles of thinking. He also specified a new form of therapy. It would not be an exaggeration to say that Beck's work has changed the nature of psychotherapy, not just for depressions but for a range of psychological problems.

In recent years the cognitive techniques introduced by Beck have been merged with the techniques developed earlier by the behavior therapists to produce a body of theory and practice which has come to be known as "cognitive behavior therapy". There are two reasons why this form of treatment has come to be so important within the field of psychotherapy. First, cognitive therapy for depression, as originally described by Beck and developed by his successors, has been subjected to the strictest scientific testing; and it has been found to be a highly successful treatment for a significant proportion of cases of depression. Not only has it proved to be as effective as the best alternative treatments (except in the most severe cases, where medication is required), but some studies suggest that people treated successfully with cognitive behavior therapy are less likely to experience a later recurrence of their depression than people treated successfully with other forms of therapy (such as anti-depressant medication). Secondly, it has become clear that specific patterns of thinking are associated with a range of psychological problems and that treatments which deal with these styles of thinking are highly effective. So, specific cognitive behavioral treatments have been developed for anxiety disorders, like panic disorder, generalized anxiety disorder, specific phobias and social phobia, obsessive compulsive disorders, and hypochondriasis (health anxiety), as well as for other conditions such as compulsive gambling, alcohol and drug addiction, and eating disorders like bulimia nervosa and binge-eating disorder. Indeed, cognitive behavorial techniques have a wide application beyond the narrow categories of psychological disorders: they have been applied effectively, for example, to helping people with low self-esteem and those with marital difficulties.

At any one time almost 10 per cent of the general population is suffering from depression, and more than 10 per cent has one or other of the anxiety disorders. Many others have a range of psychological problems and personal difficulties. It is of the greatest importance that treatments of proven effectiveness are developed. However, even when the armoury of therapies is, as it were, full, there remains a very great problem – namely that the delivery of treatment is expensive and the resources are not going to be available evermore. Whilst this shortfall could be met by lots of people helping themselves, commonly the natural inclination to make oneself feel better in the present is to do precisely those things which perpetuate or even exacerbate one's problems. For example, the person with agoraphobia will stay at home to prevent the possibility of an anxiety attack; and the person with bulimia nervosa will avoid eating all potentially fattening foods. Whilst such strategies might resolve some immediate crisis, they leave the underlying problem intact and provide no real help in dealing with future difficulties.

So, there is a twin problem here: although effective treatments have been developed, they are not widely available; and when people try to help themselves they often make matters worse. In recent years the community of cognitive behavior therapists has responded to this situation. What they have done is to take the principles and techniques of specific cognitive behavior therapies for particular problems and represent them in self-help manuals. These manuals specify a systematic program of treatment which the individual sufferer is advised to work through to overcome their difficulties. In this way, the cognitive behavioral therapeutic techniques of proven value are being made available on the widest possible basis.

Self-help manuals are never going to replace therapists. Many people will need individual treatment from a qualified therapist. It is also the case that, despite the widespread success of cognitive behavioral therapy, some people will not respond to it and will need one of the other treatments available. Nevertheless, although research on the use of cognitive behavioral self-help manuals is at an early stage, the work done to date indicates that for a very great many people such a manual will prove sufficient for them to overcome their problems without professional help.

Many people suffer silently and secretly for years. Sometimes appropriate help is not forthcoming despite their efforts to find it. Sometimes they feel too ashamed or guilty to reveal their problems to anyone. For many of these people the cognitive behavioral self-help manuals will provide a lifeline to recovery and a better future.

Professor Peter Cooper
The University of Reading

Preface

Not everyone who has suffered childhood trauma will experience significant problems in adulthood, but many men and women do struggle to come to terms with histories of hurt and abuse. Some actively seek advice to help them deal with the psychological consequences of being abused as children, while others cope alone.

This book introduces a recovery plan which has already helped many who struggle with emotional and relationship problems. It is based on the principles of cognitive behavioral therapy, which are described in Part One of the text. In our clinic, throughout the 1980s and 1990s, an increasing number of men and women asked for help in dealing with the painful aftermath of an abusive childhood. For some their trauma had been emotional, in the form of verbal cruelty and neglect; for others the hurt had been physical or sexual. The difficulties our clients faced varied from person to person: some experienced mood problems, some relationship difficulties, while others struggled with low self-esteem or a persistent eating disorder. Some found their day-to-day lives were affected to a large degree, while others seemed to be handicapped only some of the time.

With colleagues, I offered cognitive behavioral therapy to survivors of childhood abuse and, over the years, clients commented on the approach we adopted. We listened to these comments and used the feedback to improve our treatment program. In this way, we developed an approach to overcoming childhood trauma which is based on the principles of cognitive therapy and which has been guided by those who have had to come to terms with their traumatic past. Initially, this approach was only offered in the clinic as a therapist-supervised treatment; but now its principles and structure have been adapted for this self-help manual.

We know that some survivors will need professional support to help them overcome childhood trauma, but many will be able to move forward by using this text. Those of you who do decide to seek professional help will have benefited from learning more about the psychology of childhood abuse and from developing some basic coping skills.

Survivors of trauma can suffer from a range of difficulties in adulthood, but whatever the problems you face, this book aims to help you deal with the unpleasant consequences of being abused as a child. Both men and women *do* recover from the legacies of a traumatic childhood, some faster than others, some with setbacks along the way, but the struggle to overcome the difficulties from the past is worth the effort.

This Book and Getting the Most Out Of It

This book was written to help survivors of childhood trauma prepare for, and make, those changes which will then help them gain control over the sorts of problems which are common among survivors. The approach is very much a step-by-step plan which encourages you to be systematic in developing the skills you need for recovery. You can put your progress "on hold" at any time.

The steps in recovering are outlined in the contents list of the book. Although this might look like a school curriculum, don't be put off. The content and the order of issues in the self-help plan have been thought through so that they follow a natural pattern and so you can gradually build on your progress. In some ways, the experience will be like becoming a student. First, you will be introduced to the theory (Part One) and to the basic coping skills (Part Two). Once you are familiar with the "basics", you can work through key issues (Part Three). Throughout, you will be encouraged to practice what you learn, just as the language student practices conversation or the music student practices playing an instrument.

Like a student, you will find it helpful if you keep written records of your aims, your progress and the exercises that are suggested in this book. So get a notebook or a file where you can keep your notes and observations together. In this way, you will forget less and you will be able to review your progress more easily.

Part One of the book will give you the background information which you need in order to understand more about childhood trauma. It addresses what we mean by "childhood trauma," how common it is, what difficulties can arise because of it and, most importantly, how you can start to overcome problems. In order to use this book, you will need to know something about the way in which problems develop and how cognitive behavioral techniques can help, so this is also discussed in Part One. Thus, you will be able to understand how *your* particular difficulties arose and how *you* can use cognitive behavioral techniques to help yourself.

In some ways, Part One (and aspects of Part Two) are like the manual that comes with your television set. The manual contains background information and details about the different options for getting the most out of your TV, in the same way that the earlier parts of this book will help you understand and get the most out of this recovery program. It can be tempting to ignore a manual and, instead, to try to get by through trial and error. Such an approach will get you so far, but you can be unaware of the full potential of your TV – and, if something goes wrong, you can find that you don't have the knowledge to put it right. Also, if you haven't read the manual, you can make very serious mistakes. So, do read through the early sections of this book as they will stand you in good stead.

Part Two presents more of a "what to do" guide, focusing on preparing for change. You will learn essential mood and stress management skills and you will begin to build your self-esteem and learn to look after yourself, at the same time developing a better understanding of your difficulties. You will also learn ways of remembering the past without being overwhelmed by it. This is a very important section. It is not only the foundation for the rest of the work; it is also your "safety net" – a set of coping strategies which will buffer you against setbacks. I would encourage you to work on this section before moving on to Part Three.

Part Three looks at the issues that we know are relevant to survivors of abuse, issues such as: dealing with self-blame and feelings of guilt; managing anger; sorting out relationship problems and sexual difficulties. A final chapter in this section emphasizes how you can continue self-help in the long term.

The entire plan is very "active." In effect, you will be asked to take on a project, and that project is your recovery. You will be asked to read sections, complete exercises and carry on work between reading parts of the book. There are diaries to complete, practical suggestions for facing difficult situations and exercises to help you relax. We know from research that the "active" part of cognitive behavioral therapy contributes to its effectiveness, so it is important to put effort into the practical side of recovery. Having said this, it is also important that you feel free to decide what particular exercises in the book will be helpful for you, and how long you want to spend on them. If an exercise is distressing, you may choose to leave it and come back to it at a later time when you feel stronger. Don't pressure yourself unnecessarily.

Some readers might use only the early parts of the book: that's OK. Part One will increase your understanding of the patterns and impact of childhood trauma and this can be therapeutic in itself. It can also be very thought-provoking and you might decide to set the book aside at this point while you reflect on what you've learnt. Parts One and Two on their own might offer sufficient guidance for some readers to be able to cope with many day-to-day problems, and these people might choose not to move on to Part Three immediately, or at all. Some readers will find that they work through part of the recovery plan, put it on hold for a while and return to it some weeks or months later. The most useful thing you can do for yourself is use this plan compassionately – don't push yourself faster than is helpful to you, take breaks when you need them and recognize that the stresses and strains in your own life will influence the rate at which you can recover.

PART ONE

Understanding Childhood Trauma and Recovery

The first part of this book aims to explain things. This is because overcoming childhood trauma begins with understanding more about it and the ways in which people come to terms with traumatic histories.

This part of the book begins by exploring what we mean when we use the term "childhood trauma." It also describes the sort of problems that have been linked with past trauma and it looks at the different pathways that recovery can take.

Part One also explains just how any of us develops problems. This will help you to understand why *you* struggle with certain difficulties. Finally, the last chapter in this section looks at how you can use cognitive behavioral therapy to deal with these difficulties.

Try to resist reading this part of the book too quickly or superficially; time spent working through Part One is well-invested time. This section will help you to put your difficulties in context and will help you to see a way forward. You can then decide whether or not you feel ready to move on to Part Two.

What Do We Mean By Childhood Trauma?

Both survivors and helpers frequently ask this question, yet the answer remains unclear. Fortunately, recovery is about overcoming the difficulties of today and not about defining past experiences, so our lack of clarity about the meaning of "childhood trauma" shouldn't hold you back. None the less it will be useful to know the current situation with regard to defining childhood trauma and the abuse that causes it.

Defining Trauma and Abuse

There is much debate and disagreement concerning the definition of childhood trauma and abuse, and just how common it is. However, something that researchers and clinicians generally agree upon is that childhood abuse falls into three categories:

- emotional abuse
- physical abuse
- sexual abuse

In the past, *sexual* abuse was considered to be the most damaging of the three, but more recent research has shown us that all types of childhood trauma can result in difficulties for the survivor. *Emotional* and *physical* abuse do contribute to psychological problems in adulthood, and these forms of abuse should not necessarily be considered less serious or damaging than sexual abuse. Of course, many survivors will have suffered a combination of physical, emotional and/or sexual trauma and all of these need to be taken into consideration when you are trying to understand *your* current difficulties.

Disagreement arises when researchers try to define the types of childhood abuse more precisely, and at present there is no general agreement on a definition. If we consider just the research literature on child *sexual* abuse, this is defined in many ways. Some researchers use broad definitions, such as "any unwanted sexual experience during child or teen years," which would include kissing or seeing someone expose him- or herself sexually. Other researchers use very strict criteria, for example stating that sexual abuse only occurs if the victim is within a certain age range, if the act involved penetration and if the abuser was sexually motivated. You can appreciate that the experiences of many survivors of sexual abuse would not be recognized by the second definition, while some non-damaging acts could be assumed under the first. Needless to say, there are definitions which lie between these extremes. Similar problems and confusions also exist when we try to define physical and emotional abuse.

To add to the confusion, few of the definitions take into account *neglect*. Those of you who have suffered physical, emotional or sexual neglect, such that your childhood needs to be protected and nourished and loved have not been met, will realize that neglect, too, can be hurtful and harmful. The sorts of experiences which could be described as "neglect" would include a parent carelessly turning to a son as an emotional or sexual confidant before the boy is old enough to cope with this pressure; a parent turning a "blind eye" to the abuse of a child; a mother so caught up in her own problems that she is never there for her own child. For some children these experiences might be bearable, but for others the experience could be overwhelming and deeply distressing.

A carer might neglect a child knowingly or without realizing it; but, either way, there is a risk of the child suffering. Studies of children show that neglect, as well as active abuse, causes distress in children which can persist into adulthood, and which is sometimes linked with emotional problems.

How Can You Spot Abuse?

There is no typical picture of an abusive situation: boys and girls are both at risk; the victim can be any age, and the abuser male or female. Abusive acts are as various as the abuser's imagination and range from those which involve contact (e.g. physical beatings and shaking, masturbation and sexual penetration) to those which do not involve contact (e.g. starvation, isolation, humiliation and verbal cruelty, forced witnessing of sex acts, being photographed for pornographic purposes). Abuse can be intended or careless; the abuser may be close to the child (a parent or friend) or be a stranger; the episodes of abuse may be single or repeated over years; the number of perpetrators can be several; the motives of the abuser vary – some will have sexual motives, while others might seek control and power, or be driven by curiosity.

It's important to remember that childhood typically involves lots of touching and tickling and teasing which is purely affectionate, safe and loving. Very many children bathe with family members and climb into their parents' bed to find that they simply feel comforted and cherished. At a time when we are learning more about the horrors of abuse, we have to be careful not to grow paranoid about natural interactions with our children.

Of course, there are "grey" areas where it is difficult to be sure if the touching and teasing is cruel or caring, playful or exploitative. Some of you might never be sure if you were abused or not, but that doesn't mean that the possibility or the uncertainty must undermine you in some way. If you are unsure, this book is as relevant to you as it is to those who are certain of their abuse.

So what can we say about the definition of "abuse" and "trauma" in childhood? Given the many forms of abuse committed against children and young adults, it is important not to hold too narrow a view of childhood trauma. We should appreciate that recognizing and dealing with the actual difficulties that a person suffers is more important than classifying early experiences.

The *personal meaning* of the traumatic experience is very important as it is closely related to the problems a person has in adulthood. So, it is more important to think what this *meaning* might be rather than focusing too closely on the description of an abusive act. Consider the personal meaning of abuse and neglect for the two youngsters described below:

Simon was an eight-year-old at boarding school. A gifted mathematician, he was awarded extra lessons with a widely respected teacher from a nearby college. This teacher sexually abused Simon on several occasions and threatened to hurt him if he told anyone. Simon trusted his parents and was able to tell them. They immediately informed his school and the police. They supported Simon throughout the police inquiry and then took a family holiday so that he might recover from his ordeal. His experience of abuse was never a taboo subject, but the family didn't dwell on it either. As a young adult, Simon remembers the specific trauma but without shame or guilt. He also recalls a great sense of being cared for and protected by his parents. As an adult, he was able to put the experience behind him.

Suzy, at twenty, had great difficulty in trusting others – particularly men. She had not had a single close relationship and the thought of sex frightened her and left her feeling vulnerable. She related this to her stepfather's constant sexual comments throughout her late childhood and adolescence. Whenever her mother was absent, he had made sexual suggestions to her, had wandered into her bedroom when she dressed and undressed, refused to put a lock on the bathroom door and then took the opportunity to watch her bathing. She turned to her mother who dismissed this as fantasy and nonsense. As an adult, Suzy was very depressed and isolated. She felt that she was to blame for the distress that she had undergone as a youngster; she felt threatened around men and untrusting of women. She felt unprotected and confused about sexual boundaries and avoided getting into relationships.

As an adult, Simon did not experience problems related to

his terrible childhood ordeal. For him it had been a specific time of trauma which deeply upset him, but it was also a time when he realized how precious he was to his family and that he could trust those who were there to care for him. The personal meaning for Simon was that bad things can happen but he also felt safe, worthy of being cared for and protected. In contrast, Suzy really struggled as an adult. Her stepfather had never touched her, but his constant sexual infringement left her feeling vulnerable and confused, while her mother's refusal to help her convinced Suzy that she was unloved and of no importance. Furthermore, she felt afraid to trust.

In each of these instances, an objective description of events, without reference to Simon's or Suzy's interpretation and the reactions of their parents, would fail to convey the *personal meaning* of the traumatic experience.

Exercise

Rather than wondering whether or not your experiences fit a definition of "abuse," remember that abusive experiences vary widely and, instead, try to piece together an understanding of how your experiences affect you today. If it helps, make notes of your thoughts.

How Common Is Childhood Abuse?

Again, we are very uncertain about this: we really don't know how common it is. Surveys have been carried out in clinics and in the community, but the disagreements over definitions, the successful covering up of abuse and the reluctance of many individuals to report it all contribute to a poor appreciation of the extent of childhood abuse.

In the UK, the National Society for the Prevention of Cruelty to Children (NSPCC) surveyed adults and found that, in childhood, 12 per cent had suffered physical abuse, while 11 per cent had suffered sexual abuse. To give you some idea of what we know about the current likelihood of child abuse, in the UK 35,000 children are on the national child protection register because they are at risk of cruelty, 9,000 are registered as at risk of physical abuse, while 6,000 are registered as at risk of sexual abuse. Given the understandable caution of authorities in putting children on the register and given the likelihood that some abuse will go unrecorded, these figures must give us a very conservative picture.

What we do know is that children *are* abused and that some of those children will go on to have problems in adult life as a consequence of this. If you have been abused as a child and now struggle with emotional and relationship problems, you can know that you are not alone.

Key Points

- There are many occasions when touching and teasing are perfectly innocent and safe.
- However, we can't ignore the fact that child abuse does occur, even though we don't yet have precise definitions of abuse.
- Although a definition may have to be emphasized in some instances – for legal reports, for example – your main concern should be understanding the effects of your experiences. When it come to recovery, this is more important than defining the abusive experience.

2

What Problems Are Linked With Childhood Trauma?

Despite the confusions in defining and identifying childhood trauma, researchers have tried to understand just what sorts of difficulties might be associated with abuse and neglect in childhood.

Early researchers tended to look at particular problems such as eating disorders, marital problems, depression and so on. It soon became clear that no one problem stood out as being associated with childhood trauma, yet many of these specific difficulties were linked to a history of abuse. The conclusion we can draw from this is that the experience of childhood trauma increases the likelihood that a person will develop any one of many problems as an adult. Thus, childhood abuse does not cause a *particular* problem, or set of problems, but early abuse renders a person more vulnerable to developing difficulties. Something else that became clear from the research was that the more severe and repeated the experience of abuse, the more likely a person is to develop later problems.

It is important to recognize that problems in later life are *not* inevitable. Research also tells us that good experiences in childhood can build up a person's resilience. This means that some children might suffer abuse but not develop problems in adulthood because their well-being is influenced by other factors. For example, the worst effects of abuse can be offset if the child has the encouragement of a loving and caring family, or if the child has good self-esteem and does not assume blame for the abuse, or if the child is supported when and if the abuse is disclosed. If you think back to Simon and Suzy, it is clear that Simon had all these "protective" factors and coped well, while Suzy had none of them and was very much harmed by her experience of abuse.

There are some problems which seem to be especially common among survivors of abuse. These include drug and alcohol problems, eating disorders, self-injuring, social difficulties, mood and anger problems and some physical difficulties. These are summarized in Table 2.1. Such problems also occur in people without abusive histories, so do bear in mind that having these difficulties does not necessarily mean that a person has been abused.

Table 2.1:   Common Problems among Survivors of Abuse

- Alcohol and drug misuse
- Eating disorders
- Self-harming behaviors, such as cutting or burning oneself or attempting suicide
- Social withdrawal, shyness, lack of self-confidence
- Poor anger management, with difficulties either showing anger or controlling it
- Anxieties and fears
- Depression, hopelessness and helplessness
- Guilt and shame
- Some physical problems in the genital region, including painful sexual intercourse

---

Survivors of abuse can also face problems in relationships, for example, difficulty in trusting others and in developing intimacy. There might be extra strain on relationships because the survivor of abuse struggles with mood problems or withdraws to protect herself from the hurt she fears. A survivor may be a poor judge of character and find himself with another abusive person. And those with histories of sexual abuse can have difficulty in their sexual relationships. In Part Three of this book we look more closely at relationship problems.

Negative Belief Systems

A particularly important legacy of abuse is the *belief system* that a child develops and the way in which the child subsequently views its world. We all have a variety of beliefs, some emotionally positive, some negative and others neutral. For example: "I am OK" and "The future looks rosy" are positive beliefs which would leave any of us feeling good; negative beliefs such as " I am weak" and "These people are dangerous" would leave us feeling miserable or afraid; while neutral beliefs like "The sun will rise," "I have brown hair," have little emotional impact. These beliefs might be true or false, but if I *believe* that I am OK, I feel good and if I *believe* that I am weak, I feel bad.

Survivors of childhood trauma tend to have more than their fair share of negative beliefs, so their view of themselves and their outlook is more likely to be negative, too. Professor Jehu, a British psychologist and one of the first to study the belief systems of women who had been sexually abused, found that their views of themselves, others and the future were distinctly negative. His findings are summarized in Table 2.2; in view of these, it is not surprising that many survivors of abuse struggle with their mood and their relationships.

Table 2.2: Common Beliefs among Survivors of Abuse

Beliefs about self	Beliefs about others	Beliefs about the future
I am unusual I am bad I am worthless I am to blame	Others are untrustworthy Others are rejecting	The future is hopeless

In our clinic, in 1995, we carried out a simple survey of the beliefs of survivors and discovered five themes. These were:

- *"I am bad"*
- *"I am helpless"*

- *"I am unclean"*
- *"I am a misfit"*
- *"I am nothing"*

This last one described those who felt that they had no real personal identity or purpose.

Not everyone in the survey felt this way – in fact, some clients were quite positive about themselves; but these beliefs were common enough for us to see the themes emerge. Again, one is left thinking that it is little wonder that a child who has endured abuse and developed some of these beliefs is vulnerable to having problems as an adult.

Thinking Processes

In addition to showing a tendency towards certain beliefs, the actual thinking process of survivors of trauma might be subtly different in some ways. The two main findings of researchers are:

- Survivors tend to "detach," "space out" or "tune out" more than the average person (this is a common phenomenon called dissociation);
- Survivors are much more sensitive to abuse-related triggers, so that, for example, a violent or cruel passage in a book would have a stronger impact on someone who had experienced childhood violence or cruelty.

Detaching or "Spacing Out"

We all dissociate at times; it is the mental process of "detaching" and we do this to differing degrees. Sometimes it is only partial and we perhaps "drift off" a little, daydreaming or doing a task without really thinking about it. Sometimes we "cut off" from our emotions, or we don't really take in what is happening, or we don't feel quite "real." Sometimes the dissociation is more profound than this and a person can be so detached that they can't remember what's been happening; they have no memory of events.

In traumatic situations such as road traffic accidents, assault or combat, it is common for a victim to dissociate. Some describe having "out of body" experiences, others lose the memory of events. If a child is in an traumatic situation and cannot physically escape, then mental escape is the sensible option. Many abused children survive because they have been able to detach from the reality of their situation in this way.

> *As soon as he came to my room, I started to imagine myself just melting into the mattress, just disappearing . . .*

> *. . . I found myself floating away from my body . . .*

Sometimes we try to achieve dissociation because we want to be less focused, we want to detach. Most of us have tried to "lose ourselves" in a good book or by watching a compelling film, but people also dissociate through drinking alcohol, smoking, using drugs, binge eating, self-injuring, gambling and so on. All of these can help a person achieve a "tuned-out" state, but not all of these behaviors are safe, or even legal, and some can make problems worse.

Sometimes we tune into different aspects of ourselves. For example, at work a woman would tap into the professional part of herself; out with friends, she would tune into the social, playful part of herself; and when her child needed her, she would get in touch with the maternal part of herself. It's common to slip from persona to persona like this, it helps us function effectively.

> *. . . it's as if I became a separate person – a soldier who felt no pain. I wasn't Sam any more.*

Unfortunately, some people find that they slip from one facet of themselves to another so easily and so frequently that they feel as it they are not quite functioning as a single person. They might even feel as though they have several distinct personalities within them. This doesn't necessarily present a problem, but if you are worried or confused because you don't feel as though you function as a single person, ask your doctor for help or seek advice from a professional therapist.

In summary, then, dissociation is a perfectly normal response, but it can cause problems if it interferes with a person's day-to-day functioning or if attempts to achieve a detached state are harmful. In Part Two we will look at ways of tackling dissociation so that you can make it work for you.

Sensitivity to Abuse

The finding that survivors of abuse have a special sensitivity to abuse-related information makes a lot of sense, too. It reflects the strategy: "better to be safe than sorry." If a child has been abused and he is now extra aware of danger, he can better protect himself: he has a heightened awareness and he's on the lookout. If hurt is avoidable, he'll be able to escape, and if it's not, then he can prepare himself. This reaction can be carried into adulthood where, if a person is still at risk, it might be helpful. However, if there is no risk, the oversensitivity can interfere with the quality of a person's life. Again, in Part Two we will be looking at ways in which you can appraise your initial reactions so that you can be confident in weighing up a situation.

Exercise

Consider these two thinking processes, "tuning out" and being sensitive to abusive-related information.

- Do you find yourself detaching?

- When does it happen?

- Does it cause problems?

- Do you find that you are extra sensitive to certain topics?

- What, in particular, upsets you?

- Does this ever cause you problems?

Again, make notes as this will help you explore your thinking processes more thoroughly.

Traumatic Memories

We all have memories, and some are more vivid and enduring than others. Powerful occasions tend to give us our most powerful memories, and these can be pleasant recollections – such as the birth of a child, or a special birthday; or traumatic events – a road traffic accident, the death of a loved one, childhood abuse.

Memories can be like an "action replay" of events and there are good reasons why we experience this rerun of events. First, the "action replay" enables us to review the situation and learn from experience. Imagine that you nearly had an accident in your car. You would feel shaken and the memory would stay with you for some while. Having the persistent memory means that you can review the incident and you can begin to come up with a better way of driving in the future ("Next time I'll be prepared at that junction . . . next time, I'll make sure that I check all my mirrors . . . next time, I'll take it a bit easier . . ."). Secondly, by reviewing memories, we are get used to the content, so that it grows less emotionally charged. Memories of accidents and bereavements tend to get easier with time and, although we might not lose the memory, it recedes into the past and is less vivid and upsetting.

Occasionally this process doesn't work properly and memories remain vivid and painful or frightening. They can seem uncontrollable and this can make them a traumatic experience in themselves.

Some memories can seem to come out of the blue, although they are usually triggered by something. Triggers for traumatic memories can be obvious or subtle. They include sounds, the feel of a fabric, smells, certain words, being touched in a certain way or bodily sensations. The distress that they cause can sometimes lead to quite dramatic attempts to disrupt them, such as self-injury, binge eating or drug misuse. In Part Two of this book, you will learn some safe strategies for managing traumatic memories.

Survivors of trauma tend to suffer two types of problem memory: *intrusive memories* of events and vivid *flashbacks*. Sometimes, survivors experience traumatic memories in the form of *nightmares*.

Intrusive Memories

These are memories which intrude into consciousness, particularly when a person's mind isn't occupied. With this type of recall, there is always the sense that a past event being is recalled but without a feeling that the past is being relived. It's a normal phenomenon and not necessarily traumatic. Pleasant intrusions include daydreams, recalling a good film from the night before, thinking about a loved one. These don't usually bother us; we tend to be relaxed about them and they drift out of our mind again. However, traumatic memories can also intrude and, of course, these are distressing and more difficult to let go of. The more we try not to think of them, the more persistent they become.

Flashbacks

This term is commonly used to describe a particular sort of remembering which is characterized by very vivid recall. Everyone experiences flashbacks at some time and they need not be frightening. Examples might be the sound or smell of a bonfire taking us back to a happy childhood scene, or a piece of music reminding us vividly of the qualities of a friendship. However, survivors of trauma are often troubled by unexpected flashbacks of what happened to them. These can be very upsetting, particularly at night-time when the memories can be especially vivid and difficult to manage.

The experience of a flashback can take many forms. Some experience flashbacks as just a "sense" of a previous trauma, while others feel as though they are reliving the past. A flashback is not necessarily a complete memory but can reflect a single aspect of the past event, such as the physical sensation of abuse, or the sound of a voice, or the smell of a certain perfume, or a powerful feeling of danger. Flashbacks are alarming but, if you have them, remember that they are not an indication that you are going mad or are going to lose control.

Below are some descriptions of flashbacks:

> *"I have a powerful 'sense' of something familiar and upsetting, but I can't describe it in detail."*

"When I have a flashback, there are no pictures but it's very physical and I re-experience the sensations that I felt during abuse."

"I 'watch' what I went through, like seeing it on film."

"It's as if I am reliving the experience all over again."

"I have a vivid and recurring nightmare."

Although the actual incident may be some time in the past, the experience of flashback can be very immediate, very "here and now", and as such, can be powerful and frightening.

Flashbacks can be triggered by many different things, such as the tone of someone's voice; being touched in certain ways; the smell or feel of certain objects or materials; certain physical positions, seeing someone who resembles the abuser; certain words or places.

Nightmares

It's not unusual for memories or flashbacks to happen in the form of nightmares. Sometimes, the content of the nightmare replays the trauma itself, but often the dream itself is distorted or changed so that it *represents* the meaning of something traumatic. The nightmare might hold the meaning "threat," "shame" or "humiliation," for example.

How Reliable Is Memory?

There has been much concern about the possibility that we can hold "false memories" for trauma – that is, inaccurate recollections of abuse which we believe to be true. The most thorough review of this phenomenon was carried out by a committee of experts working for the British Psychological Society in 1995. The committee's conclusion was that, for any of us, *memory is largely accurate but it can be distorted or elaborated.*

It is important to remember that "memory is largely accurate," but we should recognize that, to some extent, we all have false memories: I can lose my car keys and, on reflection, recall seeing them on the kitchen table. The more I think about it, the more certain I become and I can even see this in my mind's eye. It is then a surprise when I find them not on the table but in a jacket pocket.

The most likely origin of false memory is suggestion. In the simple example of the car keys, I was subject to self-suggestion: I kept telling myself that I had left the keys on the table until I had convinced myself that it was so.

Studies have shown that some of us (but not all of us) can be strongly influenced by repeated suggestions from a trusted person. If a trusted person emphasizes that something has happened, it becomes more believable. This is why advertising campaigns use famous and trusted personalities to say good things about certain products. This suggestibility perhaps explains why so many of the claims of false memory of abuse are associated with (trusted) therapists who have interpreted abuse in their client's past.

The strong influence of suggestion can also help us to understand why abused individuals can be so unsure of their history when a parent or carer has denied or minimized the abuse. Carers and parents are trusted figures. When they say "It's nothing, don't make a fuss," or "I did nothing of the sort," or "You are lying as usual," a child doubts his own memory of events.

It is important to appreciate that sustained pressure to remember or persevering with a possibility can create false memories in some of us. The more one imagines that the keys are on the kitchen table, the stronger that memory becomes. So, one shouldn't try to force recall, for this can lead to distortions in memory; rather, one should simply allow memories to return.

The committee also recognized that amnesia, or memory loss, from trauma is reported by victims, and that recall of "lost" memories can occur both with and without psychotherapy. This supports the idea that we can repress traumatic memories and that they can re-emerge later in life. In a way, having no memory of abuse when it has really occurred is a false memory.

The message to take away from these discussions is that it is not unusual to have gaps and distortions in one's memory, but that the overall recollection is generally accurate. It's true that memories can be in error, but this usually reflects *incorrect* rather than *false* memory. Imagine two friends have taken a holiday together and a year later look back over that time. They might have a common general memory about how they spent their time, but it would not be unusual to hear: "Oh, I'd completely forgotten that!" or "We didn't, did we?" or " No, you're wrong, we went to the museum that day." All of which reminds us that memories are not perfectly accurate.

It is also important to recognize that memories are not perfectly detailed. Precise details might be missing from our recollections and yet we can still have a reliable "sense" of events. For example, when I go to the video store, I can pick up a video and know that I've seen it and that I enjoyed it (or hated it, or was very moved by it) – and yet I won't always be able to remember the plot or the ending. Sometimes I can't even remember who starred in it, and yet I still have an awareness of how I felt about the film and a true sense of what the film is about.

So, memory is a complex phenomenon: it's not as simple as having a video tape in our minds which can record and replay events. However, it is generally reliable, although not so reliable for details.

Key Points

- Childhood abuse does not directly cause problems, and problems occur in the absence of childhood abuse.
- Such abuse, however, does render a person *more vulnerable* to a wide range of difficulties.
- In particular, an abusive history can affect the way we think. It influences the way we view ourselves, our world and our future, and this affects our relationships and the way we feel about ourselves.
- Traumatic childhood experiences can also stay with a person, so that s/he might suffer from frightening memories in adulthood.
- Although our memories of childhood are imperfect and sometimes subject to suggestion, they tend to be generally accurate.

3

Recovering from Childhood Trauma

Although a traumatic childhood may have left you with difficulties in your adult life, you can expect to be able to change some things and to make your life different. We know that victims of childhood trauma do recover. We know this from research, and we know it from the many accounts of recovery that one can read in the autobiographies of survivors. We also know that, for some, making the changes will be quite easy, while others might struggle even though the motivation is there.

Anyone who decides to make any significant life change might be faced with risk-taking, difficult decisions, daunting challenges, and the boring and repetitive tasks which are necessary in learning new skills. Most people look back over that difficult time and think that the effort was well rewarded.

The ideas in this book are based on the experiences of men and women who have used our clinic. They have made changes in their lives, have faced the stresses which have arisen, have learnt new ways of coping and, in general, have told us that the struggle is worthwhile. However, you shouldn't assume that challenges and struggles are always a bad thing: some of our clients said that recovering from childhood trauma presented a really exciting challenge and one which was enjoyable because they could see the benefits and felt that they were, at last, taking control of their lives.

Preparing to Make the Change

Deciding to change is not an all-or-nothing decision. Psychologists have shown that this is a subtle process with many stages. These can be summarized as: "not even thinking about it," "thinking about it," "planning it," "getting on with it" and (hardest of all) "hanging in there." These stages are often used to understand the struggles and ups and downs associated with changes such as giving up an addiction, choosing a new career, taking up exercise or going on a diet.

You probably know a smoker or a dieter who has been at different stages of readiness to change. Consider the stages that they go through. Early on, they are not even contemplating giving up smoking or overeating ("There's no problem. I'm happy as I am" or "There's no point, I just can't do it"); then they begin to consider it ("Maybe I should try to give up; I'm not sure"); the next step is making a commitment ("I *will* stop smoking when I finish my exams" or "I'll diet when I come back from our holiday"); and eventually they actually change their behavior. That's not the end, of course, because they now have to maintain the change, have to resist the urges to give in and to go back to their old ways. Often there are setbacks and lapses, and the smoker or dieter might even find himself back at the planning stage. Generally, the most successful person is the one who believes that the effort is worth the stress it might create, who has the ability and resources to deal with those stresses, and who is living in an environment which can support change.

This is the typical pattern for anyone deciding to make a significant life change, and before you undertake to make changes in your life, you need to reflect on your stage of readiness to change. If you are in the thinking/planning stage, then you might benefit most from simply reading this book, as it will give you more information and ideas to think about and use to help you make the right decision. If you are in the "action" stage, then you'll find that you will be able to both read the book and begin to follow the practical suggestions for making changes. If you start to make changes but then find that you've taken on too much, expect to move back into a "thinking/planning" phase for a while.

The Process of Recovery

The process of recovery can vary enormously, and you need to bear this in mind when you consider your expectations and when you review your own progress. Most survivors make their recovery in stages and, as a general rule, those with more stable lives, good support and fewest difficulties will make the fastest progress because they have less to change and are making changes in a supportive environment.

Sometimes recovery itself can set up stresses, as relationships change or fears are faced, and it is not unusual to take a break from the task in order to adjust to the changes.

A common expectation is that progress runs smoothly (Figure 3.1). In fact, most people find that their progress is much more likely to be stepped (Figure 3.2), with times of obvious improvement and times when things seem to plateau.

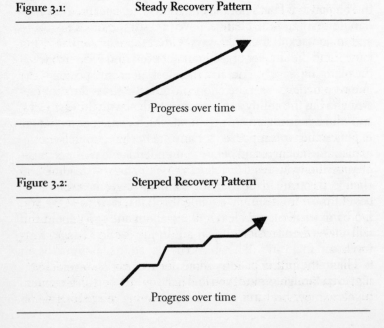

Figure 3.1:   **Steady Recovery Pattern**

Progress over time

Figure 3.2:   **Stepped Recovery Pattern**

Progress over time

Another common pattern is a series of ups and downs, as in Figure 3.3. In this case, progress feels as though it is made up of two steps forward and one step back.

Figure 3.3: **Erratic Recovery Pattern**

Progress over time

The patterns shown in Figures 3.2 and 3.3 can leave a person feeling demoralized during those times when gains aren't obvious. In fact, each of the three patterns represents progress, but each shows a different rate of improvement and gains over time. So, you will need to stand back and ask yourself: "Am I really getting nowhere, or have I simply hit a plateau for the time being?" Or: "Am I really back at square one, or is this just a hiccup in my progress?" If you have hit a plateau, or if you are experiencing a temporary setback, there will usually be an explanation. For example, you might have made so many changes that you need to "rest" a while to consolidate and get used to your achievements; or you might have taken on a bit more than you are ready to cope with at that particular stage. Do try to understand the fluctuations in your progress, as this will make them easier to bear and help you to keep looking forward.

There is a further pattern of recovery which is worth describing, even though some of you will not experience it. This pattern involves a person having a sense that things are getting worse before they get better. This is a common experience for those who have kept things bottled up for years, or who have suppressed memories which then begin to surface. Survivors of abuse can find memories returning after years of being dormant. This can be shocking and distressing, but you should recognize that it is normal. In fact, it can be very beneficial to recall the past, as remembering is often beneficial to recovery.

Sometimes these memories are of entirely "forgotten" events.

"You know, I had no idea that he'd hurt me in that way. I never liked him and wondered why, but I didn't realize what he'd done. It came back to me suddenly and many things fell into place."

Sometimes an actual event is not forgotten but the emotion linked with it was numbed. This emotion can return, and fear, hurt, shame and shock can resurface long after the abuse has ended.

"I always knew that I'd been abused, but it was as if it meant nothing to me. If you'd asked me about it, I could have rattled off the details without feeling anything. In the last year, I've started to feel pain and shame when I remember my abuse. This feels more normal but it hurts, now."

Sometimes it is a case of a misread event becoming clear with time: a man might realize, for example, that his mother wasn't really unaware of his abuse but that she turned a blind eye.

"When I was at school, I believed him when he said that I was special and that's why we had our secret. I actually felt special. I would let him do anything because I trusted him. Imagine my shock when I read that he'd been arrested for molesting at least four schoolgirls. He was nothing but a sick teacher who took advantage of me and abused me."

Whatever form these recollections take, they can cause pain and misery – and, for a while, a person can feel worse than ever. This is shown in the first part of Figure 3.4, the "recollection" phase.

Figure 3.4: Recovery Pattern Where Things Worsen Before They Improve

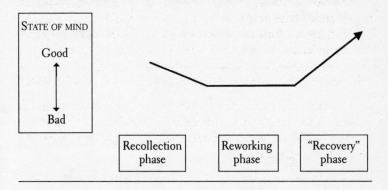

Although it is painful, the benefit of enduring this stage is that those who go through it retrieve their history and can begin working through it, coming to terms with the shock and forming a new understanding of themselves. This next stage is the "reworking phase." During this time a lot is happening in terms of progress, even though some feel here that they've hit a plateau with regard to their mood. Once this middle phase is achieved, we tend to begin to see a more typical "recovery" pattern, as shown in Figures 3.2 and 3.3, and it becomes easier to see that there really is light at the end of a tunnel.

If you find yourself in the "recollection" phase and you feel that your mood is getting very low, I would advise you to seek support from your GP, a trained counsellor or a psychotherapist. Expert support, and sometimes medication, can make this phase more bearable and will help reassure you that it will come to an end.

Key Points

- One can recover from the effects of childhood trauma, but sometimes one has to wait until the time is right to start to make the necessary changes in one's life.

continued on next page

- Change can be made in stages: you can take on the task step by step, getting the pace right for yourself, giving yourself time to adjust.
- Progress almost always involves "ups" and "downs," so be prepared for this.

4

How Problems Develop

The Early Days

To some extent, the scene is set at our birth – we are all born with our own temperament. Some of us are naturally placid, some feisty, some timid, some seemingly fearless. From the beginning of infancy, we interact with our environment – the people and the things around us – and we have many experiences. Our experiences, combined with our natural temperament, then shape our personalities, our ability to deal with stress and our vulnerability to problems.

It is not unusual for a child who has a secure, loving childhood to develop into a self-confident adult who can relate well to others, while the child who has suffered neglect and trauma might feel uncertain of himself and his future, and struggle to develop lasting relationships. Research carried out in the 1960s, by a psychologist called Bowlby, showed that infants have a powerful need to be cared for, both emotionally and physically, and if this care is constant and predictable the infant will develop a real sense of security and confidence. In adulthood, she or he will be able to form good relationships and not be afraid of getting close to others, nor worry unduly about being abandoned. Such people have a basic trust in themselves and in others.

In contrast, infants who have an unpredictable or unstable carer, a carer who is abusive or neglectful, or who gives mixed messages and cannot be relied upon, often lack confidence in themselves and in others. As adults, they might be overfearful of being abandoned and hurt, and have difficulty trusting. They may try to cope with the fear by clinging to a partner and seeking much reassurance, or by avoiding close relationships altogether. Sometimes insecure adults experience a distressing combination such that they both cling to and reject partners in an attempt to protect themselves from hurt. This often puts stress on a relationship and can contribute to problems in friendships or a marriage, for example.

A child's early experiences and relationships influence its sense of self, its outlook and its view of the world in general. A boy who experiences stability and caring is likely to form a balanced view of himself and hopeful picture of life, while a boy with a traumatic history can develop a negative view of himself, of others and of the future.

Children are very good at learning things, and this is a great advantage in their development and survival. In particular, children are good at learning from adults such as parents, family friends and teachers. Children are "primed" to believe these people. Some adults give encouraging and honest messages that help a child to develop a healthy and balanced view, such as "I am loved," "I matter," "I can achieve things if I try," or "I can form friendships."

Abusive adults, however, can give messages that leave a child confused, insecure or self-critical. Unfortunately, if a child or a young person learns something that is not true, she or he can carry a false belief into adulthood, which can cause problems for the adult. Often, these beliefs echo the words of the grown-up, and one can almost hear the adult's voice in the child's conclusion: for example, "I am bad," "I don't matter," "I am a liar," "I am stupid," "I can never be safe," or "I only do things for attention." Some beliefs gained in childhood have a significant impact on relationships with others: for example, "No one can like me," "I can trust no one," or "I must please others all of the time."

Children try to make the best sense of their world. They try to understand painful and frightening experiences as well as they can, but without the guidance of concerned adults, their conclusions can be biased. Often, children assume that if bad things happen it is because of them, and conclude: "*I* am bad" or "*I* am weak" or "It's *my* fault." Children tend to see themselves as helpless and, without reassurance, will assume: "There's no point in trying" or "Others *will* hurt me" or "Something terrible *will* happen."

The particular type of unhappy event that children experience also affects their outlook. With significant *losses*, children can grow pessimistic, feel hopeless and be more prone to depression. The more *stresses and trauma* children have, the more likely they are to see the future as frightening and themselves as at risk – which can give rise to many anxieties and fears. Without a secure environment to help them develop a more objective view, this negativity can persist into adulthood.

On a positive note, happy childhood events, support and reassurances all contribute to a child's self-confidence and a healthy optimism. Even the child who suffers trauma can be buffered against its harmful effects if that child also has some stability and good relationships in her or his life. You know that you suffered trauma as a child, but did you also experience some caring and stable relationships, and did you have good things happening in your life? It is important not to neglect your healthy experiences, as these can contribute to your recovery.

Fortunately, one's self-concept and patterns of relating to others can change. A person can become more confident, learn to trust and develop more healthy relationships. In order to do so, it helps to understand why the problems might have arisen in the first place and what beliefs early experience gave rise to.

Throughout this book, you will see personal beliefs being categorized as:

- beliefs about self
- beliefs about others or the world
- beliefs about the future

These beliefs are often referred to as *core* beliefs because they are so fundamental to our sense of ourselves and the world we live in. They influence our every thought, feeling and action, so we all benefit from being able to identify them. Some of them will be positive, some negative, some true and some false. In Chapter 13, you will find out how you can learn more about your belief systems and you will learn how to re-appraise those that are not so accurate.

Exercise

Reflect on your early experiences and consider the balance of helpful and unhelpful experiences and relationships that you've had.

- How might this affect you now?
- How has this affected your view of yourself?
- How has this affected your view of others?
- How has this affected your view of the future?

Belief Systems and "Mental Filters"

Childhood is a time when we build up systems of key beliefs, some of which are held with great conviction and are usually associated with strong feelings. Belief systems can reflect very healthy convictions, such as:

"I have rights and I deserve respect from others" or

"No one should treat me badly" or

"I am basically decent and likable."

However, the belief system is not always positive and is not always accurate. Some survivors of abuse carry around beliefs like these:

"I am vulnerable and everyone is out to get me: I won't trust anyone."

"I am worthless and will never be loved."

"I can do nothing to protect myself, so there's no point in trying."

"I must always please others so that they don't grow to dislike me and reject me."

Although such beliefs *feel* true, some are very inaccurate indeed. Over the course of this book we will be looking at this type of belief system more closely.

These belief systems act as "mental filters." Everyone's view of their everyday experiences is shaped by their belief systems. Imagine three women with different "mental filters":

- *Doris* believes that she is not a particularly nice person, that sooner or later, others will realize this and they will abandon her;
- *Annie* believes that she is basically an OK person but that bad things happen to her and that the world is a dangerous place;
- *Olivia* sees herself as basically OK, and reckons that most people are trustworthy.

Each has arranged to meet a new friend in a café. The friend doesn't turn up on time, and each woman's "mental filter" influences the conclusion she draws:

- Doris assumes that her friend has thought better of the friendship and has abandoned her, so she leaves;
- Annie's first thought is that something terrible has happened to the friend and she orders a drink to calm her nerves;
- Olivia thinks that there is probably a good reason for the friend being late and wonders if she has the friend's mobile phone number.

The net effect is that Doris is distressed and hurt, Annie panics, while Olivia keeps calm and is able to think of ways of resolving the situation.

Some of our belief systems reflect the truth: Olivia is an OK person, the world is a dangerous place at certain times, certain persons might be untrustworthy.

However, some belief systems *feel* as though they must be true but in fact are not. Once people believed that the world was flat, and most children believe in Santa Claus; but as modern adults we realize that these are misconceptions. Doris's belief that she is not a nice person is a misconception, as is Annie's belief that the world is always a dangerous place – it is true that Doris is not perfect and that the world is dangerous at times, but both women overestimate the negative.

We can re-evaluate our "mental filters" and we can change them, but this takes time and a great deal of effort. Dr Padesky, an American psychologist, has likened unhelpful, inaccurate or exaggerated "mental filters" to prejudices. She suggests that a prejudice is a belief that is held with conviction as though it were a truth but which, in fact, might not reflect the truth. Anyone who holds a prejudice has great difficulty in realizing that it is only an opinion, a preconception, a certain view *which could be inaccurate*.

Exercise

In order to get a better grasp of how these belief systems operate, Dr Padesky suggests that you think of someone you know who has a prejudice – one with which you disagree. Maybe that person is racist, or sexist, or supports a different football team or political party.

- Think how strongly that person holds the prejudice: do they ever question it?

- Now consider what happens when she or he discovers something that fits in with the prejudice. How does s/he react?

- What happens when she or he comes across something that contradicts the prejudice?

Very often, one finds that:

- prejudices are held with conviction
- information which fits with the prejudice is accepted and believed
- information that does not fit is ignored, rubbished, minimized and generally not accepted

These elements of prejudice are summarized in Figure 4.1.

Figure 4.1:   **How a Prejudice Is Maintained**

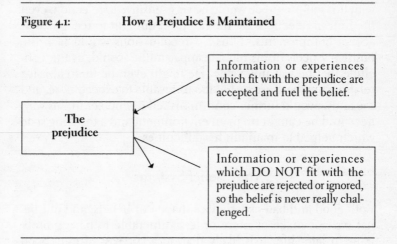

The prejudice

Information or experiences which fit with the prejudice are accepted and fuel the belief.

Information or experiences which DO NOT fit with the prejudice are rejected or ignored, so the belief is never really challenged.

In this way, prejudices are maintained without ever being challenged or questioned. This was the case for Doris, who interpreted a friend's lateness as confirmation of rejection, and for Alice, who interpreted the same situation as confirmation that the world was a dangerous place. Interestingly, both accepted their conclusions without checking out the evidence. Only Olivia thought to take action to clarify what might be happening.

A prejudice is even more likely to be maintained if a person only mixes with like-minded people. For example, we tend to read the newspapers which support our political views; we join clubs of people who tend to think as we do. It is natural to live our lives according to what we believe is true; and so it is understandable that Doris left the café in order to deal with her distress, and that Annie tried to calm her nerves as best she could.

Living according to mistaken beliefs is the most powerful way of keeping those beliefs intact. How many people do you know who think very little of themselves and, because of this, give up easily and don't try to achieve more? The subsequent lack of success then reinforces the view of themselves as unworthy. Imagine that the mistaken belief is "I am unlovable." A man with this self-prejudice would be very sensitive to rejection, even the hint of rejection, yet might find it difficult to recognize or accept compliments. Thus his recollections would lack the positive aspects of his relationships and he would, again, conclude that he was unlovable. He might even be in an abusive relationship, because he felt too unlovable to expect more, and the abuse would further confirm his self-prejudice. In this way, he would be caught up in an environment and a thinking style which helped to maintain his difficulties.

Your Belief Systems

Both good and bad experiences shape our beliefs, and our belief systems make us more or less vulnerable to having problems in later life. It is likely that, as a survivor of childhood trauma, you will have had some non-traumatic influences in your life, and it is beneficial to hang on to the positive experiences. However, it is also important to acknowledge how childhood abuse has affected your life, while remembering that not all adult difficulties are rooted in experiences of childhood abuse and not all abusive experiences cause later problems.

Exercise

First, consider your memorable experiences: good and bad. Write these down.

For example: *I was always put down and criticized by Dad; I had to keep family secrets; the men in my family were especially violent . . .*
Yet: *My teacher always encouraged me and gave me hope; I learned to struggle against the odds; I had some good schoolfriends and some fun times; I won a music prize;*

continued on next page

Sandy and I have always been really close friends; I've always been able to enjoy caring for others.

Then think how these have coloured your outlook as a adult: your view of yourself, others and the future. Again, write these thoughts down.

For example: *I have no self-confidence; I feel isolated; I am sexist; I live my life by "shoulds" and "oughts"; I avoid feelings; I can't cope; I do not trust myself; I cannot take praise; I always assume blame; the future scares me . . .* Yet: *I am determined to recover; I don't give up, something within me keeps fighting; I have a sense of humour; I do have talents; I am loyal; I am a gentle and caring person.*

It is not always easy to identify these sorts of beliefs, so don't be disappointed if you find them difficult to put into words. It might be easier if you break down the task and consider how you view yourself, how you view others and then your outlook for the future.

I am: ....

Others are: ....

The future is: ....

Next, reflect on how this leaves you feeling and how it might influence the way you deal with life.

For example*: I am always afraid; I get angry easily; I am sad; I am often depressed; I feel inferior to others; I often feel used in relationships; I can't trust others; I don't enjoy sex; I hurt others; I am not assertive; I tend to withdraw and give up easily; I seek comfort in drinking.* Yet: *I can sometimes feel positive and strong; I can communicate well, I can work hard at things; I am honest with others; I do a good job; I have protected my children*

continued on next page

from abuse; I am good at caring for others; I am determined to do something with my life.

To make the task easier, think how your belief systems affect your mood state, your relationships and the way you behave, and how this might render you more or less vulnerable to difficulties.

My mood: ....

My relationships: ....

My behavior: ....

Now you have begun to build up a picture of the link between your experiences and your belief systems and, in turn, how your belief systems link with difficulties in your mood, your relationships and your behavior. You have begun to answer the question: "Why me?" (See Figure 4.2). At this stage it is important not to dwell exclusively on the negative consequences of your experiences; note too what strengths and assets you can draw on to help you overcome these problems.

Figure 4.2: **The Answer To "Why Me?"**

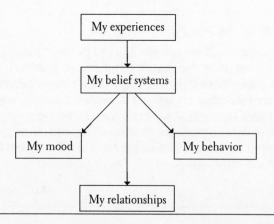

Key Points

- Both our natural temperament and our experiences influence our strengths and our vulnerabilities.
- Experiences, in particular, influence our beliefs about ourselves, others and the future.
- Some belief systems are accurate and helpful, while others may not be accurate and can cause distress.
- It is important to try to take a step back and ask yourself: "Is this entirely accurate or might this be a misconception that I need to challenge?"

5

What Keeps a Problem Going: The Five Elements

By now, you will have a better idea about the origins of your difficulties, so the next question to address is: "Why don't some of the difficulties just go away?"

For any of us, some problems resolve themselves, while others are persistent. You need to identify your persistent problems and then spend some time analyzing what *maintains* them: what stops them from simply going away?

Difficulties can persist for many reasons:

- *Our thoughts (or mental images)* which are linked with our belief systems or "mental filters"

JANE'S PROBLEM: RELATIONSHIP DIFFICULTIES. As a result of being betrayed, Jane has difficulty believing in others and trusting them – she has a "Don't trust" mental filter. As a consequence of this, she avoids getting close to anyone. By behaving in this way and never getting close to others, she never disproves her belief: she never gives another person the chance to show that they are trustworthy. Her beliefs, or thoughts, and her behavior keep her problem intact and she never lets herself form trusting relationships.

JACK'S PROBLEM : LOW SELF-ESTEEM. As a result of being abused, Jack believes that he is "bad" – he has an "I am bad" mental filter. This belief is so powerful that he only ever notices events which are consistent with his belief and he never really notices when things happen that don't fit in with his belief. Therefore, he continues to feel certain that "I am bad." His "mental filter" keeps his belief intact, which keeps his self-esteem low.

- *How we feel*: our mood, our emotional responses

TONY'S PROBLEM: DEPRESSION. As a result of being neglected and hurt, Tony is vulnerable to depression. Anyone who is depressed sees the world and themselves in a negative light – this is a typical symptom of depression – therefore, he always sees his situation and his future as hopeless and himself as worthless. His depressed outlook and critical self-appraisal continue to fuel the depression, so you could say that his mood keeps his problem going.

- *What we do*: our behaviors, our reactions to things

CLAIRE'S PROBLEM: FEAR OF LEAVING THE HOUSE ON HER OWN. Claire felt that she had never been very confident. As she grew older, she seemed to get even more insecure and she chose to stay at home, rather than go out either independently or with friends. This solitary behavior had two effects: first, friends stopped asking her out, so she had no encouragement to leave the house; and secondly, the more she avoided going out, the harder it became. The less she went out the less confident she became about venturing away from home.

- *Our biology*: fluctuations in our body chemistry

CARY'S PROBLEM: BINGE EATING AND DRINKING. Cary suffered emotional cruelty as a child and she learnt to eat for comfort. As a adult, she still tries to block out pain through binge eating and drinking. This, initially, gives her great comfort because eating and drinking both affect the body's chemistry and make us more relaxed. Thus, she "eats and drinks" her way through painful episodes in her life, but she never learns to deal with pain, so the next time a crisis arises, she binges to cope. Her problems are maintained by biological and behavioral cycles.

- *Our circumstances*: the way we live and work

FRANK'S PROBLEM: SHYNESS AND SOCIAL ANXIETY. Frank was

bullied at home and at school. He grew into a very socially timid man who believed that he was useless and dull. He lives with his parents; he has a job and a few good friends who tell him that he is good company and make efforts to include him their social plans. The actions of his friends help Frank to question his assumptions about himself; but when he goes home, his father criticizes and bullies him while his mother stands by, as she has always done. Once again, Frank is left believing that he has nothing to offer. Although his friends help him to challenge his old belief system, his home environment revives it and he remains a timid, anxious adult.

Each of these examples describes cycles which serve to maintain problems. You could, perhaps, start to think about your own situation and what cycles might prevent you from resolving your difficulties. Over the course of this book it should get easier for you to find responses to the questions "Why me?" and "Why isn't the problem going away?"

These are not easy questions to answer as many of us find that our problems are difficult to analyze; so, at this point, you need only to *begin* considering your difficulties. We have not yet finished exploring the cycles that maintain the problems.

As we keep seeing, problems are *complex*, and reflect the interplay of different aspects of ourselves and our environment. When you try to tease out the different aspects of your problem, remember the *five elements* which we have just looked at in the examples given above:

- *your thoughts (or mental images)* which are linked with your belief systems
- *how you feel*: your mood, your emotional state
- *what you do*: your behaviors, your reactions to situations
- *your biology*: physical changes and fluctuations in your body chemistry
- *your circumstances*: the way you live and work, what is happening around you.

This may sound very complicated – and to some extent it is – but Dr Padesky and her colleague Dr Mooney helpfully summarized this interlinking of the five elements. They use the model shown in Figure 5.1 to illustrate just how intertwined these aspects of our experience are: thoughts and images, feelings, behaviors and biology all impact on each other and further interact with the environment in which we live. At any one time, our experience is the combination of this "network."

Figure 5.1: **The Interlinking of the "Five Elements"**

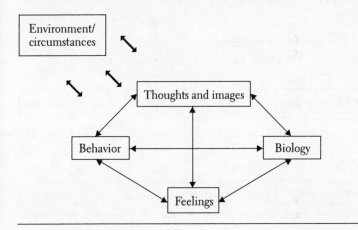

This diagram is actually less complicated than it might at first seem, because we can take each element in turn and see how it relates to the others.

You might be wondering why we need to tease apart these elements. It is helpful to do so because each link in the model offers an opportunity for change. In fact, changing one of these elements often has an impact at several levels. For example, cognitive therapy research has shown that addressing the thoughts and images within the "network" will influence not only a person's thinking style, but also the way that person feels and behaves. The more familiar you are with your "network," the easier it will be to identify and break the cycles that keep your problems going.

Thoughts, Feelings and Behaviors

As we saw in the examples, these aspects of our experience can interact with each other; thus cycles are set up, and so problems can become persistent. The cycle that interests cognitive therapists, in particular, is the "thoughts and feelings" cycle. We know from years of research that the way we feel affects the way we think, and the way we think affects the way we feel (see Figure 5.2). Our mood is affected by what's on our minds and our state of mind is influenced by our mood.

Figure 5.2:   The Links Between Thoughts and Feelings

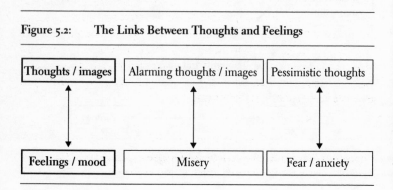

Thoughts / images	Alarming thoughts / images	Pessimistic thoughts
↕	↕	↕
Feelings / mood	Misery	Fear / anxiety

Imagine that you are at your friend's wedding and you are having the best possible time. The thoughts that fill your mind are probably very up-beat, positive thoughts and the memories that you recollect in conversation are most likely to be warm, happy ones. This will keep you in good spirits and, as a result, your thoughts and memories will continue to be in a positive vein.

Now imagine that you are watching a scary film. You are tense and your anxiety level is high. The screen doesn't have to show a frightening image when you hear a noise; your mind will take care of that. In your mind's eye you will "see" the murderer or the ghost because you are already anxious. These images will fuel your fear even further and you will be more prone to thinking the worst.

A similar pattern is experienced with depression. Every depressed person feels miserable, and research has shown us that the more unhappy a person is, the more negative or pessimistic is their thinking. In turn, negative thinking deepens the misery and then the depressed person is prone to further unhappy thoughts and memories. It is no wonder that it is sometimes very hard to break out of depression.

The way we think and feel also influences our behavior (see Figure 5.3). A wedding guest who is feeling happy and confident will be outgoing and, as a result, invite more social interaction; and so he will continue to have an enjoyable day. The scared person typically runs from, or avoids, that which she fears, and so the fear goes unchallenged and she remains anxious, imagining the worst. The depressed person is likely to become more withdrawn in his behavior. In doing so, he is less likely to get a sense of achievement or pleasure from his world and this can help to keep the depression going. He is then even less likely to overcome his social withdrawal.

Figure 5.3: The Links Between Thoughts, Feelings and Behavior

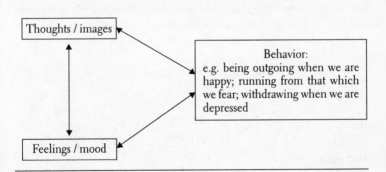

In addition to these links, the way we think and feel and behave is further influenced by our physical state (or our biology) and by our environment (or the circumstances in which we live and work).

Biology and Environment

The biological and environmental aspects of our experience are just as influential as our thoughts, feelings and behavior, although *biological* elements can be particularly hard to pinpoint.

Our Biology

Our biological state, though often hard to define, can have a very powerful effect on the way we feel, think and behave. We know that there are very clear biological or chemical changes associated with anger, depression, stress, hunger, fear, elation, excitement, craving, illness, medications and so on.

These biological states directly affect the way we feel. For example, if you are depressed, you can *expect* to experience certain symptoms such as tiredness and loss of enjoyment as well as the misery which is characteristic of depression; if you have just suffered a viral illness, you might *expect* to feel run down, rather low and tired; if you are under stress at work, you can *expect* to have stress-related symptoms such as tense muscles, poor concentration and agitation. If you are hungry, you can *expect* to feel tense and irritable; if you have a hangover, you can *expect* to feel fragile and to be muddle-headed. Most women are familiar with the emotional and physical changes that are associated with menstruation. Again, these are triggered by biological fluctuations.

An important chemical in our bodies is a substance called adrenaline. It is this which makes us feel agitated when we are anxious, hungry, angry or simply excited. Because this same chemical is associated with anxiety, hunger, anger and excitement, it is easy for us to confuse our feelings. This means that we can assume that we are agitated and afraid when we are actually hungry or angry, or we can think that we need something to eat when in fact we are angry, not hungry. If you are not used to expressing feelings like anger, it is easy to assume that your agitation is caused by something else; if you are used to feeling afraid, it is easy to assume that all feelings of agitation reflect fear.

A final word about adrenaline: it is stimulated by caffeine – and that's why we can feel uplifted or wound up by a chocolate bar or a cup of coffee. It is wise not to have too much caffeine as this can lead to unpleasant feelings of agitation, and if you are prone to anxiety or angry outbursts, high caffeine levels will only make matters worse for you.

Food, alcohol, drugs and self-harm trigger different brain biochemicals, and the effect can be very comforting. The chemical changes often give immediate relief, and so overeating, drug and alcohol misuse, and self-harm can be very addictive. However, in the long term, they almost certainly make the situations worse and it's advisable to find alternative ways of achieving comfort. This is not easy, and we will address this question again in Part Two of the book.

Some medications can bring on euphoria or misery, so it is always a good idea to ask your doctor to explain the emotional side-effects of any drug treatment. Certain medical conditions, particularly hormonal ones, can also affect the way a person feels and behaves. So, if you have a physical problem, again remember to ask your doctor about the emotional impact that this might have.

As far as you can, take the biological element into account when you are trying to understand your problems. The advantage of this is that you avoid blaming yourself for reactions which might be perfectly "normal," given your biological state.

The Environment

The fifth aspect of our experience that merits close consideration is the environment we live in. This includes our home, social and work circumstances. Since the 1970s, we have known that the amount of stress which we experience in our day-to-day life affects our well-being. Put simply, the more stress we have to deal with, the more likely we are to struggle with emotional problems.

We can be stressed at home as well as at work; in our social life just as easily as in our professional life. And stress can take many forms. It can arise because of a single stressful event: a house move, a job change, the end of a relationship, an illness or a financial crisis, for example. Alternatively, it can arise because of a series of more minor events coming together at once, such as a minor illness, some changes at work and a disagreement with a close friend. Or it can arise because of concerns which last for some time: poor housing, chronic financial difficulties, a nagging and critical close relationship, unsatisfactory working conditions, a physical problem that isn't getting any better.

There are two good reasons for recognizing stress in your life. First, you can acknowledge the part it plays in your difficulties, rather than simply blaming yourself for your struggles. Secondly, you can ask yourself if there is anything that you can do about it. Some stresses we have to accept and tolerate as best we can, for example learning to live with a physical disability, or adjusting to caring for a sick relative. There are other stresses which we can resolve by taking practical steps to get help – steps such as seeking financial advice from a bank, visiting a doctor to ease physical problems, using a counsellor to help with relationship difficulties.

Some stress we have to recognize as being partly of our own making, and we can try to change some aspects of our own behavior in order to ease that stress. A classic example of this is the "workaholic" who overworks, gets tired and stressed by this, but continues to take on too much. She needs to change her behavior and reduce the amount of work she takes on. Another common example is the person in a stressful relationship, who is so tense or angry that he can't be civil to his partner and so their relationship suffers all the more. Alternatively, a person may be in a stressful and critical relationship and so worn down by it that she adopts the position of "doormat" and becomes even more of a target for criticism and emotional abuse. In these instances, the stressed person needs to become more assertive, opening up the possibility of breaking the cycle of a worsening relationship.

You might be thinking that this is all very well in theory, but it's not so easy to put into practice. You would be quite right, and in Parts Two and Three of this book you will learn more about the strategies you can use to break some of the more difficult cycles.

In order to illustrate what we have been saying in this section, here are two examples of the way in which problems might develop and how the five elements interact. In both cases, it is this interplay which maintains or keeps a problem active.

> *Susan had a tendency to get depressed. She found her work stressful (ENVIRONMENT) and this had worn her down so that she began to feel rather depressed (FEELINGS). As her mood changed, she found that she had less energy to do things (BIOLOGY) and she began to neglect social and leisure activities (BEHAVIOR). Her social withdrawal meant that she no longer engaged in the activities which she used to find pleasurable (BEHAVIOR) and her depression deepened (FEELINGS). She began to think: "What's the point?" (THOUGHTS) whenever her friends encouraged her to join them and was in danger of becoming quite reclusive.*

> *John had relationship problems. One evening, he had arranged to meet a friend in the snack bar at a local gym. Ten minutes after the agreed time, his friend had not shown up (ENVIRONMENT). John's conclusion was: "He's let me down. Another person who's taken advantage of me. I'm not standing for this!" (THOUGHTS). As he thought this, he felt a surge of adrenaline (BIOLOGY) and he slammed his fist on the table (BEHAVIOR). By now he was enraged (FEELINGS), and when his friend walked in, John was rude and did not listen to the friend's explanation for his being late. John stormed out of the gym (BEHAVIOR) having seriously damaged this friendship (ENVIRONMENT), but unable to act differently because he felt such fury (FEELINGS). Later, he reflected on his action and regretted the hurt he might have done to his friend (THOUGHTS) – after all, he did not have many friends and this saddened him (FEELINGS).*

The advantage of clarifying reactions in this way is that a pattern can be interrupted once it is understood. For example, Susan could try to alter her environment by decreasing stress at work and increasing her social activities, and/or she could try really to remain active rather than withdrawing and doing less, and/or she could analyze and try to challenge her negative thinking pattern. Similarly, John could try to catch, analyze and challenge his angry thinking pattern, and/or he could try to modify his behavior so that he did not offend his friend and did not leave situations before a resolution could be found.

Key Points

- Our experience, at any one time, reflects several elements: the way we feel, how we think and what we do, and the influences of our biological state and our environment.
- These elements interact and influence each other. For example, the way we think affects the way we feel and vice versa.
- The problems that we have can also be understood in terms of this "network," and we can begin to tackle our problems by identifying the different elements of the "network" and by attempting to change some aspect of it.

6

Putting Your Difficulties in Context

The first step in applying what you have learnt in the previous chapters is understanding just what makes up your difficulties: what is it that *you* think, feel, do and experience that creates problems for you.

Identifying your own "five elements" will be difficult at first because you are unlikely to be used to analyzing your reactions in this way. However, it does get easier with practice, and diary or record keeping can help you tease out the different aspects of a problem situation. As you better understand the different aspects of your difficulties, you will better appreciate what keeps them going or what maintains them.

To help you do this, there is a diary at the end of this section. Use this to help you identify the relevant aspects of your experiences. Note when you are feeling distressed or when you feel particularly good. Then, try to describe your circumstances and, if you can, catch the thoughts or images that were going through your mind. Also note what you did in response to your feelings.

When you can identify the things that are running through your mind, you will find it easier to make the links between your thoughts, feelings, behaviors and your situation. As with most things, the more you practice this, the easier it gets.

Exercise

- Try to keep a diary for several days.
- Then look back over it and see if you can spot how many

continued on next page

---

of the day's problems or upsets are a result of vicious cycles of distress, or of unhelpful patterns in your responses.

- Don't just concentrate on the bad aspects, though: look out for the things that you do which ease the situation or put an end to the problem.
- Eventually, you will find that you can build on these helpful responses, while trying to decrease the unhelpful ones.

Learning to analyze your experiences can be therapeutic in itself. Often one feels less puzzled or less stupid when it is possible to say : "No wonder this keeps happening." However, this is only a first step and, from all that we've said about maintaining cycles, it's probably obvious that recovery involves learning to break those patterns. There's no doubt that this is often very challenging because breaking familiar cycles means risking change, and also facing the consequences of change. As this is something that deserves more consideration, we will be looking at the implications of deciding to change in Parts Two and Three. For now, you should just concentrate on developing your skills in analyzing your reactions.

There are more blank diary sheets in the Appendix at the back of this book.

A Word About Diaries and Record-Keeping

Mention diaries or record-keeping and most people groan. In our clinics, we frequently encounter the client who hasn't kept records or who is filling in a week's worth in the waiting room, reminding us that this is not a task that feels familiar or easy. Keeping records requires effort, it's time-consuming and it's not always convenient.

However, there are significant benefits to keeping records of your experiences as they happen. The real advantage of this is that you can catch feelings, thoughts, actions and situations as they happen, before poor memory can distort things. Then you

Diary 1

Monitor your feelings each day, noting when you feel upset or particularly good. Jot down what was happening at the time. Then, see if you can catch what was going through your mind and note what you did. Note these details as near to the time of the distress as you can – it is easy to forget later!

Date/time	EMOTIONS How I felt	ENVIRONMENT What was happening at the time	THOUGHTS OR IMAGES What was going through my mind	BEHAVIOR What I did
Monday	Lousy	The computer crashed and I lost hours of work	This always happens to me: life is unfair. I'm stupid for not making copies earlier.	Cursed. Gritted my teeth
	Really good	Curled up on the sofa with a funny novel.	I feel safe and cosy. This story is cheering me up.	Stayed where I was, getting more relaxed. Later bought another novel by the same author

have a realistic picture of your experiences. Over time these pictures begin to add up and you will be able to see patterns. Once we understand patterns, we can identify maintaining cycles and we can make predictions; once we can make predictions, we can begin to break unhelpful patterns. This puts you in control, but you must collect reliable information in the first place.

Consider this example, taken from the business world.

A store manager is aware that a department is losing money. He has three options:

- He can make random changes in that department, without reflecting on his experiences of that department, but then his chances of solving his problems are low.
- He can base changes on his recollections of the department, but some of his memories might be hazy and he might have overlooked important issues.
- He can record what is happening in the department, as it happens; then he can look at the figures and patterns and base his decisions on these facts.

The most effective approach would be the third. The manager would have collected information which would allow him to see exactly what was going on in the department. His "data" would be reliable.

In recommending that you keep records, I am suggesting that you operate like the manager who collects facts and figures before making important decisions.

Understanding *Your* Problems and Needs

This section is dedicated to understanding even more about *your* difficulties and *your* needs. Later, you will be taking steps to meet those needs by making changes in your life. Again, you will be looking at the questions "Why me?" and "Why aren't things getting better?" and then you can reflect on what you need to do to begin to make changes in your life.

"Why Me?"

Although overcoming childhood trauma is about dealing with present difficulties, an appreciation of their origin can make it easier to understand "Why me?" That then makes the task of dealing with today's problems easier.

By now, you probably have a clearer appreciation of psychological problems: what renders a person vulnerable to them and what keeps them going. Remember that not all adult difficulties are rooted in experiences of childhood abuse and not all abusive experiences cause later problems. Don't assume that, because you have been abused, you are bound to have problems, or that having problems will always link back to an abusive history.

It is easier to answer the "Why me?" question if you describe each of your current difficulties, and then tease out all the factors that contribute to each difficulty. Below is an example to help you start thinking about this.

> *Janice first described her problem as "I'm unhappy and I can't stand it – but I blame myself!" The more she reflected on this, the more she realized that there were, in fact, two aspect to her unhappiness: she had difficulties in maintaining relationships and she was prone to bouts of depression. The more she considered her problems, the more she realized this, and that she wasn't directly to blame.*

Problem 1:   *I can't get on with others for very long.*
Why this is understandable: *My family was so hostile and uncommunicative that I never learnt how to communicate and feel at ease with others. I don't believe that I can trust them. I have so much tension and anger bottled up inside that I don't always treat others respectfully. After I was abused I felt dirty and shameful – I still believe that I am bad – so I'd rather not get close to anyone in case they see the real me.*

Problem 2:   *I feel depressed a lot of the time.*
Why this is understandable: *All the criticism and hurt left me feeling very bad about myself, I really believe that*

I am unlovable and that I don't matter. So, I get miserable just being me. The abuse that I suffered stays with me in my memories and the constant reminder brings me down. My childhood was unhappy; I've learnt how to be depressed but I don't know how to get out of it and I don't believe that I can. I have no confidence in myself.

By doing this exercise, Janice came to appreciate that her unhappiness wasn't the result of a weakness in her character or of being too stupid to sort herself out: there was an alternative, plausible explanation that gave her hope that she could change the situation.

Exercise

- Identify your current difficulties, and for each consider why it is understandable, in the light of your earlier experiences, that you struggle with a particular difficulty.
- Try to be as compassionate and understanding towards yourself as you would be towards a friend.
- Remember, you are only just embarking on this "project" of recovery, so don't be disappointed if the task is too taxing right now.
- At this stage, you simply need to start thinking about possible links; you can always come back to the exercise at another time.

"Why Aren't Things Getting Better?"

If a problem is persistent, there is always an explanation, even though it can be difficult to pinpoint at first. The question "Why aren't things getting better?" takes us back to the unhelpful cycles that we discussed earlier. In general, unhelpful cycles explain why things aren't improving.

The advantage of being able to identify cycles is that they tell you what needs to be changed. For example, if a person can't get along with others and identifies the unhelpful cycle of *avoiding social contact* as being a major maintaining factor, it is clear what needs to change: however challenging it is, the person needs to create social contacts.

In Part Two, we will look at ways of making the necessary changes in order to break unhelpful patterns. At this stage, you are just considering why things aren't getting better. In Janice's case, it was because of the following reasons:

Problem 1:   *I can't get on with others for very long.*
What maintains this: *I have no social skills so I avoid social contact. Therefore, I never learn to be at ease with people. I have no idea how to control these feelings of tension, so I keep offending others and driving them away. I'd rather not get close to anyone in case they see the real me, so I keep away from people and I'm not able to form friendships.*

Problem 2:   *I feel depressed a lot of the time.*
What maintains this: *I really believe that I am unlovable and that I don't matter. So, I avoid being with others and that means that I've only got myself for company and that depresses me. I don't know how to manage the memories so they are a constant source of misery. I have no confidence in myself, so I don't mix with others and I don't do anything enjoyable. I never have fun or do things that seem to cheer up other people.*

Although this did not solve Janice's problems, it directed her thinking towards areas where she might make changes.

Exercise

Again, you might find it helpful to write down your thoughts about maintaining cycles as in the example of Janice above.

"What Do I Need Now?"

Now you have thought about explanations for your current
problems, you can translate these into your current needs. For
example, you might need more time to learn to trust someone
because you are more vulnerable to being hurt by criticism than
others are. You might need to learn to be more assertive; or you
might need encouragement to develop a social life.

Janice decided that these were her needs:

Problem 1:   *I can't get on with others for very long.*
What I need: *To learn social skills so I stand a better chance
of getting on with others; to learn how to control my feelings of tension, so I don't drive others away; to build my
self-esteem so I can form friendships.*

Problem 2:   *I feel depressed a lot of the time.*
What I need: *To build my self-esteem, think better of myself,
so that I am better company for myself and so that I can,
perhaps, make some friends; or to learn how to manage
the memories, to be more active, so that I stand a chance of
getting some enjoyment out of life.*

Exercise

- Once more, try writing down your needs, as Janice did
  in the example above. You can then use your notes for
  reference when you need to review your needs.
- As this list is likely to change as you work through this
  book, it is important that you remember to review it from
  time to time.

By now, you will have begun to clarify your difficulties and to
understand where they come from and what keeps them going. The next step is addressing the question: "What can I
do?", and this takes us on to the subject of cognitive behavioral
therapy.

Key Points

- Understanding the important elements of your difficulties will require some analysis, and a diary or record-keeping will help you to achieve this.
- Then you can begin to answer the questions: "Why me?", "Why aren't things getting better?" and "What do I need now?"

7

How Can Cognitive Behavioral Techniques Help?

At this point, you might be wondering: *just what is cognitive behavioral therapy?* Cognitive behavioral therapy, or CBT, is a talking therapy which aims to improve mood and change unhelpful behaviors by tackling the thoughts, memories, images and beliefs which are linked with problems. We have already seen that adverse experiences tend to give rise to problem belief systems and CBT is ideally suited to tackling them.

The therapy itself was developed in the 1970s by Aaron T. Beck and is now a well-established therapeutic approach which has been shown to be helpful with a wide range of mood, stress and behavior problems.

You will be familiar with the framework which underpins CBT as it's the one we have been using to understand the origins of your problems and what keeps them going (see Figure 7.1). The term "cognitions" refers to thoughts, images and beliefs, namely the things which run through our minds.

As you know, this model links the past with the present and, although we can't change the past, people can learn to live a fulfilling life despite the trauma they have undergone, and CBT can help them achieve this. At the end of this book (p. 211) is an epilogue written by a woman who used CBT to overcome lifetime difficulties. You might find it an inspiring testimony to read before you embark on your own journey of recovery.

Figure 7.1:   Understanding the Origin of Our Difficulties

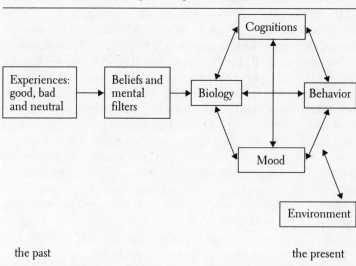

the past   the present

Why Consider Cognitive Behavioral Techniques?

A particular strength of cognitive therapy is that it has always been evaluated through research. This research has shown that, although present difficulties comprise the elements of cognitions, mood, biology, behavior and environment, we can make reliable changes to the whole system by putting our efforts into addressing the cognitions and behaviors – hence the term cognitive behavioral therapy. This means that if a person tackles his or her unhelpful thinking patterns and problem behaviors, mood and environmental improvement tends to follow.

Clinical trials have shown that CBT has proved helpful to survivors of abuse, and many other trials have established it as an effective therapy for several of the problems associated with childhood trauma, such as depression, anxieties, eating disorders and relationship problems. Although the early trials used therapists, more recently CBT has been shown to be really useful as a self-help therapy.

In order to use cognitive behavioral techniques we need to be able to analyze our reactions and then tease out the five different elements. This is exactly what you have been doing by using the diary from the previous chapter. The automatic thoughts and images that you catch when you are distressed can then be reviewed; and, with practice, you can begin to re-evaluate them and decide how accurate they are. If they are accurate, then you can act on them; if not, you can correct them and, very probably, relieve your distress. This is a simple concept that is often difficult to put into practice, but there are a range of techniques to help you do this. We will look at them in detail in Chapter 13, "Getting a Balanced Perspective."

To get an idea of re-evaluation in practice, imagine a woman who is faced by a dog. Her automatic thought is: *"I am in danger!"* and, understandably, she feels fear. She then takes a moment to review this thought and concludes:

> *"I really don't like the look of this animal. I think that he could bite. I need to back away immediately."*

In this case, if her immediate thoughts are accurate, the feelings of fear are appropriate and this will motivate the woman to get to a place of safety.

On the other hand, she could review her first thought and conclude:

> *"I'm over-reacting because I was once bitten by a dog, and I'm still very sensitive. There's actually no real sign that this is a dangerous animal – I'll just walk by calmly."*

In this case, the initial thoughts were not accurate; they were influenced by her previous fear of dogs. This time, the fear was unnecessary and it will go away when the woman has calmed herself and gets on with her journey.

By learning some simple *cognitive* strategies, you will be able to reliably distinguish between the accurate and the less accurate automatic thoughts. You can then use *behavioral* techniques to help you to "test out" your conclusions. In the second example, the woman tested out her new conclusion by walking past the dog: that was what we call a "behavioral test."

This simple *cognitive behavioral* combination is a powerful one: not only do you develop an accurate perspective, but you back it up with action.

Although the idea behind CBT sounds simple, using cognitive behavioral techniques can be challenging. There's no doubt that getting the most out of CBT requires application, skill development and risk-taking.

You might or might not be at the right stage of readiness to start making changes and taking risks: only you can decide. If you are unsure, read through Parts Two and Three of the book, asking yourself if now is a realistic time for you to follow the program. Even if you decide that it's not the right time, you will still have benefited from learning much more about your difficulties and, whenever you feel ready, you can take the next step.

Key Points

- Cognitive behavioral techniques can help you manage your difficulties by giving you a framework for catching and evaluating the thoughts and images (the "cognitions") that underpin your problems.
- When you have appraised your cognitions, you can check out your conclusions through "behavioral tests." You can put your thoughts into action.
- You can anticipate improving your difficulties simply by focusing on the cognitions and behaviors that are linked with your problems.

PART TWO

Preparing for Change

Part Two, the middle section of this book, will take you through steps which will help you prepare yourself for change. It's a good idea to read through a chapter before trying to do the exercises, so that you can first familiarize yourself with the approaches, and then you can work through at your own pace. When you have worked through Part Two, it is up to you if, and when, you choose to move to the final part of the book. The work that you have done and the skills you have learnt will be useful to you, whatever your decision.

Although survivors of trauma can experience very different problems from one another, many of their key issues and fundamental needs are similar. So, in this section, there are some common guidelines for preparing for change. To begin with, you will need to reflect on the obstacles to change and, in particular, think about your worries or fears about recovery. Then you need to consider what you want from recovery, namely, what your aims or your goals are.

To help you in making changes, this section will introduce you to a range of practical coping strategies, including some techniques for managing problem memories. Having a good self-image is a great advantage in recovery, and later in Part Two you can also begin to work on improving your self-image and looking after yourself. Finally in this part of the book, we will begin the real "cognitive" work as you build the skills necessary to develop a balanced perspective on your life.

8

Obstacles to Recovery

Essentially, there are the obstacles that come from within us, such as fears and doubts, and there are those that arise from the outside, such as life stresses and relationship problems. It is important that you take stock of your personal worries about changing and take a good look at your current situation. If you have many other life stresses, then you might need to consider taking it slowly and not expecting too much of yourself. Ask yourself: "Right now, do I have the necessary support, at work or at home, and the emotional resilience I need?" If the answer is "No" or you are not sure, consider working through Part Two of this book without moving on to Part Three until you feel more secure.

The Stress of Change

Oddly enough, another common obstacle is progress itself. All change is stressful and even the most positive changes can create stresses, which can set you back. This is one of the reasons why progress is rarely smooth but tends to happen in a series of "ups and downs." You really do need to be prepared for these stresses, which can affect not only you but your family and friends, too. Your progress, with its emotional and behavioral changes, can lead to improvements but also tensions in friendships and marriages.

If you are a parent, try to consider the impact of your progress on your children. Often, relationships with children improve, but it is possible for a parent to become neglectful or overprotective when s/he is working through personal and painful issues. A child might find this difficult to understand. In short, keep your home life on the agenda and only take on what you can hope to manage.

In the worst case scenario, change could create tensions that put you at risk, and you must monitor this very carefully. A typical example is the person who becomes more confrontational or assertive towards an abusive partner or family member, and subsequently antagonizes that person. If this happens to you it could, at best, improve a poor relationship, but at worst, it could end an important one prematurely, or even put you at risk of physical harm.

Stirring Up Emotions

Many find that the work of recovery stirs up powerful emotions. This is often associated with reviewing traumatic experiences. For those who have spent a lifetime detaching from, or avoiding, "feelings," facing them can be disturbing.

Recovery sometimes comes with startling revelations, such as: "He didn't really care for me after all" or "I really thought that I could trust her, and I can't." Try to be prepared for strong emotional reactions and recognize that a period of "grieving" might be necessary before you can move on.

Over time, your view of the world and yourself will change and this can be shocking or upsetting. Consider the following two survivors:

Alice, in late middle age, successfully challenged the belief: "Men cannot be trusted." After an adult life of avoiding relationships and shunning intimacy she was, at last, able to begin dating and form intimate relationships. The close relationship that she had hoped for at last seemed possible; however, she now had to face the grief of having "lost" her chance of having children.

Richard, who still lived with his parents, had always believed that his father was a good man and that he had abused Richard only to discipline his son. In the course of

his recovery, Richard recognized that his father's acts had
been bizarre, cruel and unnecessary. Although it had helped
Richard to recognize that he had been abused and that his
depression was linked with this, it shocked him to have to
label his father "an abuser" and he found it impossible to
remain in his parents' house.

Exercise

This is not a quick exercise, but one to which you will have
to give much thought and which will take time.

- Reflect on your life circumstances and honestly look at
  the stresses which you, and those around you, might
  face when you take steps to create a different lifestyle
  for yourself.
- The idea is not to put you off change, but to help you
  prepare for it so that you minimize the stress and hurt to
  yourself and others.

Emotional Numbing

If you have tended to avoid "feeling" by keeping yourself busy,
distracting yourself, or using food or drugs to numb emotions,
then you could find it especially distressing to "feel" so much. If
this does happen, try not to give up prematurely and try not to
use harmful ways of coping such as hurting yourself or misus-
ing food, alcohol or drugs. Recognize that getting in touch with
more of your emotions is part of your progress. Take it easy,
pace yourself and try to develop some safe, soothing coping skills
to get through the distress. Chapter 10 will help you to build a
wider repertoire of coping skills.

Behaviors such as overwork, substance misuse, overeating or
self-harm tend to cause "emotional numbness." When a person
is sober and/or less preoccupied, emotional pain tends to surface, and you should anticipate this. Some find it easier to "tail

off" these potentially damaging behaviors, thereby *gradually* allowing more emotions to surface. If you tend to resort to coping strategies that are not good for you in the longer term, read through Chapter 10, "Building Up Your Coping Skills," to increase your options.

Exercise

- Are there ways in which you numb your feelings?
- How do you do this?
- What are the feelings (or thoughts) that you try to avoid in this way?

Worries About Change

It is very usual to have worries about making changes, even if one feels that change is for the better. Some people do actually look forward to the task because it is an opportunity to work on and overcome problems, while others feel nervous or apprehensive. Some have very mixed feelings.

Exercise

Try to identify your fears and write them down, for example:

My worries and fears about recovery:
- I am afraid that I won't be able to control my feelings.
- I am afraid that I'll have to address things before I'm ready.
- If I change, my relationship will suffer.

Identifying your fears is the first step towards overcoming them. Once you have named your worries, you can begin to consider solutions. If you can, discuss your worries with someone whom you trust – a friend might be able to help. Again, keep a record of your ideas for possible solutions.

Exercise

Look back over the list you drew up in the previous exercise and try to come up with some solutions, for example:

Overcoming my worries and fears:
- I will pace myself to avoid being overwhelmed by my feelings and I will learn ways to calm and soothe myself.
- I can decide when I'm ready to move on. This isn't a race.
- My relationship might change, but this could be for the better. I will always talk things through with my partner so that we can continue to work on our relationship.

The Gains and Losses of Change

It takes great courage to decide that the time has come to face the past and recover from its effects on you. Although there may be many gains, the process of recovery can be difficult, and you might feel that there are some losses in leaving behind the "familiar you."

We only make significant changes in our lives when it really seems worth taking the risk: when the gains that we anticipate outweigh the losses that we expect. Sometimes, from the outside, a situation can seem confusing: "Why doesn't she leave him when he treats her so badly?" or "Why doesn't he give up the drink – everyone can see that it's killing him and harming his family?" The answer might lie in what each has to lose. Perhaps the woman loses a home she's fought to create, she loses the father of her child, she loses the hope that the relationship could ever work and perhaps she anticipates living in greater fear because of his threats. Perhaps the man loses his opportunity to feel "one of the guys" instead of a misfit, he loses the one way in which he escapes from the painful memories of his past, he loses the only way he has discovered to feel relaxed around others rather than ashamed.

Some examples of gains and losses are:

What I have to gain	*What I have to lose*
The ability to control my anger	My false front, and the comfort that gives me
Self-respect and self-acceptance	My defensive barriers to hide behind
Trusting others more	My distance from others which helps me feel safe
Taking charge of my life	Being the person who pleases everyone, always, and avoids conflict

---

Exercise

In this exercise you can take time to review the gains and losses involved in recovering from the past. This will help you appreciate why the process of recovery is such hard work, and then you can make a realistic commitment to healing.

List your gains and losses. When you have weighed up the pluses and minuses, you may be clearer about your reasons for choosing to recover and you may be more aware of the obstacles in your way.

Review your list and think what resources you have to help you to tolerate the losses and the changes.

- Have you friends to help you through the most painful times?
- Is there someone to support you if you give up an addiction or leave an abusive relationship?
- Can you face the consequences of not pleasing others?
- Can your children or your partner or your close friends cope with the changes that you plan?

Again, the purpose of this exercise is not to put you off change, but to help you anticipate the realistic struggles so that you can plan to succeed.

Key Points

- Recovery involves significant changes for which you must be prepared.
- Change itself is stressful and you need to consider whether or not you are ready to deal with the stress, how far you are able to go and whether those you care about can support the changes that you plan.
- Although recovery is usually liberating and empowering, it can also stir up buried emotions and shocking revelations and you will need to give yourself time to adjust to this.

9

Deciding What You Want

This is a short chapter, but the subject merits its own section because it is so important that you are clear about what you want. Deciding what you want is about defining your goals, clarifying the direction that you want to take and what you hope to achieve. In doing this, you need to be specific: unrealistic or vague goals are rarely achieved.

Make Your Goals Realistic

Remember that goals *must* be realistic, so it is worth spending time reflecting on the possibility of your hopes. Try to avoid targets that are hopeless, like unrealistic weight loss, impossible jobs, unlikely romantic relationships. We all might want such things, but these might not represent achievable goals. If you are realistic in your aims you will not be disappointed but, instead, pleased with your achievements.

For example, some survivors want to:

- stop feeling guilty about what happened
- be able to have a trusting relationship with others
- be less afraid of sex
- feel comfortable in their own skin
- learn to manage anger
- be able to tell another what happened

Be frank and consider what personal or practical problems you will still have to deal with even if this book helps you. For example, financial problems, weight problems, a difficult marriage, worries about your children, frustration in your work might remain. If you are unsure in your choice of goals, talk things through with someone you trust.

Exercise

Set aside time to consider what you want and then review your ideas, deciding which of your goals are realistic and which need to be modified to make them realistic. Be honest about the problems that you might still be left with.

Make Your Goals Concrete

In describing your goals, be as specific as you can, so that you know what you are aiming for and when you have achieved it, or when you are off target and need to take stock again. This means that you need to ask yourself: "How will I realize that I have achieved my goal?", so that you have some concrete means of estimating your progress. Over time, you will be able to review your list to see how far you have moved towards achieving your goals.

For example, if someone had a goal of "weight loss," the markers of progress would be easy to establish. This person could simply use a reduction in pounds or kilograms to evaluate change. If the goal was "improving my relationship," then the markers are not so clear. What could a person observe to evaluate progress? In some relationships, a marker could be the number of rows that happened, fewer rows indicating progress. In another relationship, the observable marker could be time spent together, or time spent talking with each other.

Goals like "feeling better about myself" are even harder to evaluate. In this instance, a person would have to ask the question: "What would I see/others see which would show that I felt better about myself?" The answers to this would vary from person to person, but useful markers might be: "The time I spend socializing with others"; "The number of days that I don't feel depressed about myself"; "The number of compliments that I give to myself"; "The number of new challenges that I take on (however small)." Each of these criteria is concrete, so it would be possible to evaluate progress by keeping a record of them.

Exercise

- Clarify your hopes for recovery. How do you want things to be when you've done the work? Everyone wants things to be "better," but how exactly do you want to change?
- If you were to realize: "I've done it. I've recovered from my past, I can take charge of my life. I am OK," how would you know that you had recovered? What would have changed in you and what would you be doing differently?
- Use this picture of yourself to help you identify your goals for change and the "markers" that you can use to recognize the change.

Make Your Goals Manageable

Some goals might be achieved rapidly, while others will take longer to accomplish and, indeed, will only be attained in a series of planned stages. For example:

- A shy man might come up with the goal of "Signing up for an evening class." This might be something that he can tackle in a single step, or he might need to break it down into a series of steps, as he steadily builds up his confidence by first checking out the building where the classes are held, then signing up for an introductory session or very short course before tackling a busy full term's program.
- A woman who is having problems with her boss, but who finds it difficult to assert herself, might be able to summon up all her courage and confront the boss straight away, or she might have to work up to this by gaining some confidence in

being assertive with less threatening figures; then she might need to practice what she wants to say to her boss. Thus, she would gradually develop the confidence and the skill that she needed to be assertive.

So, once you have defined your goal and made it concrete, you will have to ask yourself if it is attainable in a single step, or if you need to work up to it in several stages. For example, a man might devise the concrete goal of "losing 20 pounds," but he is not going to achieve this in a single step – he will only reach his goal in a series of small amounts of weight loss. A socially anxious woman might devise the goal of "going out more with friends" and she might have made this concrete: "going to the midsummer party with my colleagues from the office." However, she may need to take this gradually as she builds up her social confidence. Her plan could look like this:

- Meet my best friend, Sally, at the cinema (I'm under less pressure to make conversation!)
- Meet Sally for supper and get used to chatting
- Meet someone from work: go to the cinema
- Meet someone from work for supper
- Go out with Sally and friend from work for supper
- Invite Sally and two friends from work over for supper
- Have a small party including friends from work (all planned and under my control!)
- Go to the midsummer party with friends from work

The woman in this example would take one step at a time. When she felt comfortable with the first step, she would move on to the next, and so on. It doesn't matter if she repeats a step a few times, because she is aiming to build up her social confidence and repeating steps will help her to do this. If, at any time, she doubts whether she can progress to the next step, she can play safe and turn the task into two smaller steps.

The golden rule in planning your progress is: *Don't take on too much – if in doubt about your ability to tackle something, break it down in to smaller steps.* You will still get there in the end, but you can do so by building on a series of achievements, rather than risking an avoidable setback.

Exercise

- Write down your goals – remember that you can always revise this list later – and put a mark by those that you suspect will have to be achieved in planned stages.
- Then go back to these and see if you can work out the steps that you need to follow.

Key Points

- In planning what you hope to achieve, there are three points to remember: make your plan realistic, concrete and manageable.
- If your goals are achievable but ambitious, don't give up on them but break them down into steps which are manageable.

10

Building Your Coping Skills

Working on early traumatic experiences can be painful at times, despite support and encouragement. One way of dealing with this is to learn to be caring towards yourself and to develop good coping skills. You will already have coping strategies that you turn to when you are stressed or upset.

Coping strategies tend to divide into those that are helpful in the short term, but which aren't healthy long-term solutions, and those which usually take more effort but are really useful long-term coping strategies. Examples of solutions which can be helpful in the short term, but might leave you feeling worse later, are:

- getting very drunk
- taking out your bad feelings on someone who did not deserve it
- hurting yourself in some way

Behaviors which might leave you feeling good about yourself over a longer time include:

- talking things through with a friend
- taking a walk
- taking a relaxing bath
- reading a book
- listening to soothing music

To help you think in more detail about your day-to-day distress and how you cope, you will find a printed record sheet on p. 78. This will help you to identify when you get upset and the coping strategies which you tend to use. Later you can review your coping strategies and decide which of these are most useful to you.

Recording Sheet: The Way I Cope

Try to monitor your levels of distress each day, noting when you feel particularly upset. Jot down what set off the distress and, so that you can judge change, give yourself a rating for how bad it feels. Use the simple scale, below, to rate your distress. Note what you did in response to the feeling upset. Then, in order to see how well your coping strategy worked, re-rate your distress levels.

1	2	3	4	5	6	7	8	9	10
No distress, calm				Moderate distress					As distressed as possible

Record all those occasions when your rating is 6 or more. Note these details as near to the time of the distress as you can – it is easy to forget later!

Date/time	Rating	What was happening at the time?	What I did in response to the feelings	Re-rating
Monday Noon	8	*Waiting for my prescription. The chemist was so slow!*	*I ran out of the pharmacy without my medication*	7
Tuesday 3.30	7	*Saw my cousin with her children and thought that I'll never be able to have a family like that*	*I talked with her and she told me that she had some problems, too. She was very kind and understanding*	4

The recording sheet gives you an opportunity to clarify just what was happening when you were stressed or upset, and just how upset you were. Then you can note what you did in response to the distress and you can re-rate your distress. In this way, you can rate the effect that your coping strategies have on your levels of distress. There are more of these sheets in the appendix.

Exercise

Use the recording sheets to analyze how you care for yourself at present. List the things that you do for yourself when you are upset, for example:

- Spend money that I haven't got
- Try to take my mind off things with a good book or video
- Take it out on those I care for and then regret it
- Turn to food or alcohol

Next, go through your list and mark with a cross (x) those behaviors which are going to make you feel worse in the long run, and then note those which are more helpful as long-term coping strategies.

By keeping records and analyzing your responses, you will learn what suits you best, and eventually you will be able to compile a list of helpful coping strategies. Some of them will be useful in a general way and some might be helpful only in certain situations. Start making your list as soon as you can, and keep on adding to it as you learn more about your stresses, reactions and what works for you. The more strategies that you have, the better equipped you will be to deal with stress.

At this point, don't expect to abandon your "short-term" coping strategies. The overall plan is to increase your range of "long-term" coping strategies so that you have a variety of ways to care for yourself when you are in distress, and you will not need to turn to the "short-term" strategies so often.

To help you expand your coping skills repertoire, the next section describes some basic stress management skills.

Basic Stress Management Skills

Anxiety, tension and stress are common triggers for distress, so this section introduces some basic stress management skills: relaxed breathing and an exercise in brief physical relaxation. You might find that learning to relax helps you deal with stress in a way that won't leave you feeling worse later. There are many relaxation exercises, ranging from lengthy deep relaxation procedures through to brief techniques which take only a minute or two; here you will learn a brief and simple exercise.

Breathing Exercise

When we are under stress, we all tend to breathe faster; but breathing too quickly, or *hyperventilating*, causes physical discomfort which can increase stress and set up an unhelpful cycle. You can stop stress from worsening by slowing down or controlling your breathing, and you will find it relaxing in itself.

"Controlled" breathing is gentle and even, without gulping or gasping. It involves using your nose and filling your lungs completely. Try to avoid breathing from your upper chest alone or breathing with your mouth open. It is generally easier to do this exercise lying down rather than sitting. When you can feel the difference between shallow and deep breathing, you can try the exercise sitting, standing or moving around.

- Place one hand on your chest and one on your stomach.
- As you breathe in through your nose, allow your stomach area to swell. This means that you are using your lungs fully. Try to keep the movement in your upper chest to a minimum and keep the movement gentle.
- Repeat this, trying to get a rhythm going. You are aiming to take about eight to twelve breaths a minute: breathing in and breathing out again counts as one breath.

At first you may feel that you are not getting enough air, but with practice you will find this slower rate is comfortable. It is important to practice whenever you can as you are trying to develop a new habit which will only come through repeating this breathing exercise.

Exercise

- Try to practice the breathing exercise several times a day.
- If you need a regular reminder, put an eye-catching mark somewhere noticeable, like your watch. You could use a dab of bright nail polish, for example. Each time you see the mark, check your breathing style and get it under control.
- Don't worry about breathing like this all of the time; if you do it several times each day, you will develop the skill.
- When you have developed the skill, you will find that you can "switch" to controlled breathing whenever you are feeling tense and this should ease the tension.

Simple Relaxation Routine

This is a short and quite simple exercise to help you relax. If you use a soothing, restful image or sound during the routine, you will relax even more effectively. This can be:

- a sound or word which you find relaxing, such as the word "calm" or the sound of the sea
- a particular object which is restful, perhaps a picture or an ornament which you especially like
- a scene which you find calming, such as a quiet country place or a deserted beach

You may need to try out one or two different words or images in order to discover what works for you. The key is finding something which suits *you*, whether this is skiing, lazing on a beach, stripping a car engine, walking through an art gallery or even hoovering.

To do the exercise:

- Sit in a comfortable position with your eyes closed. Imagine your body growing heavier and more relaxed.
- Breathe through your nose and become aware of your breathing. As you breathe out, think of your sound or image, and breathe easily and naturally.
- Don't worry whether or not you are good at the exercise, simply let go of your tensions and relax at your own pace. Distracting thoughts will probably come into your mind. Don't worry about this and don't dwell on them, simply return to thinking of your mental image or your breathing pattern.
- Keep this going for ten to twenty minutes. When you finish, sit quietly with your eyes closed for a few moments, and then sit with your eyes open. Don't stand up or begin moving around too quickly, as you may feel a little dizzy.

With practice, you will be able to respond to physical stress or worrying thoughts by relaxing, almost automatically. In order to achieve this level of skill, however, it is necessary to practice two or three times a day.

Exercise

- If you can, use this simple relaxation exercise two or three times a day.
- One of the best ways of making sure that you practice is forward planning. Decide when you will take ten or so minutes to do the exercise and note the time in your diary, so that you have made a commitment to a regular regime.
- If you have difficulty falling asleep or relaxing if you have woken up in the night, try using this exercise in bed.

Spacing Out

One consequence of early abusive experiences is that many survivors learn to deal with emotional and physical pain by distancing from it or "spacing out". This can make a person feel unreal, or as if she or he has no emotion. While this can be an effective way of dealing with extreme distress in childhood, when we have very few other coping strategies, spacing out as an adult can sometimes prevent you from resolving painful memories and feelings.

Some people find themselves distancing or withdrawing when certain topics are raised in conversation or in the media. They lose concentration and later realize that they have missed the opportunity to deal with something important.

Exercise

If you are prone to spacing out as a way of coping, try to become more aware of this and, if you are able to "catch" yourself, you should eventually be able to take control.

You can actually use your ability to space out to make it easier for you to face difficult topics. When you feel yourself distancing, try to focus on the difficult issue for only a short while and space out if, and when, you need to. As soon as you are able, try gently bringing yourself back to the topic. You have the option of emotionally distancing yourself again, if you need to. With repeated practice, it should become easier for you to stay with issues which you had felt too scared to face.

Forging Relationships

One of the greatest assets that any of us can have is social support. When we are under stress, those of us with friends and people to confide in cope best. As we have already discussed, survivors of abuse can struggle to establish and maintain friendships and they can find trusting others very difficult. Because it can be so difficult to forge relationships, Chapters 16–19 are dedicated to helping you improve your communication with friends, family and loved ones. If it helps, skip ahead and read through these chapters now, before you move on.

Key Points

- You will already have some coping skills at your disposal. Monitor them and work out which are helpful in the long term, which are only helpful in the short term and which are actually harmful to you.
- Plan to expand your coping repertoire so that you can be less reliant on the unhelpful strategies.
- Recognize the importance of social support and, if necessary, begin making plans to improve your social network.

11

Managing Problem Memories

As we saw in Part One, there are two types of problem memories: flashbacks and intrusive memories. Both types can sometimes intensify as you work on your difficulties. This is not unusual, and indeed can indicate progress: the memories will eventually lose their pain and associated emotional intensity when you work through them.

If you are having flashbacks, remember to use your coping strategies. You may also find it helpful to share your experiences with someone whom you trust, as they may have advice on how to cope. If you are able, tell someone close to you how they might recognize that you are having a flashback and tell them a word or gesture which you think will interrupt the memory.

There are three ways of managing flashbacks:

- planned avoidance
- distraction through "grounding"
- reviewing the flashback thoroughly: facing the fears it holds

These strategies can also help you to manage nightmares and intrusive memories.

Planned Avoidance

If your problem memories happen episodically, try to identify what triggers them and consider avoiding those situations or persons for the time being. The purpose of this is to give you some respite; later, when you are feeling confident that you can cope with the memories, you might choose to face these difficult situations.

Grounding Techniques

This is an approach based on distraction which aims to help you "switch off" the distressing memory by directing your attention elsewhere. It is well established that, although we can pay scant attention to a number of things, we can only really attend to one thing at a time. If this is something neutral or, better still, pleasant, then we can't also give our attention to the unpleasant memory.

Strategies which might help you are:

Refocusing Your Attention

This requires you to concentrate really hard on something in your environment: for example, the shade and texture of curtains, the feel of the arms of a chair, the titles of books on the shelf, a passage from a book which you carry around with you. In order to achieve distraction, you will have to concentrate very hard: don't just settle for "the chair is green," but look at it more closely. Is it textured? Is it fabric or plastic? Just what shade of green is it? How would you describe the shape? Look at it as if you were a detective at the scene of a crime.

Exercise

Try to do this now. Focus on the things around you; discover how easy or difficult it is for you. Practice doing this even when you are not struggling with problem memories, so that you get skilled at refocusing.

Using a "Grounding" Object

This idea came from a group therapy member in the mid-1980s. She discovered a grounding object for herself and found it so effective that she told the rest of the group. The other group members then chose grounding objects and, similarly, found them really useful in a crisis.

So what is a grounding object? It is a comforting, tangible object which can distract you when necessary. In order to achieve this difficult task, the object must fulfil one main criterion: it must be something that carries a positive meaning for you. Clients in our clinic have, for example, bought themselves cute soft toys, wooden or alabaster eggs, pretty scarves, handsome key fobs, elegant card cases and so on. It is also good to choose something portable, something that you can carry around with you and squeeze when you are in distress to bring you back into the present. When you hold your grounding object, you will need to use your refocusing skills to ensure that the object works as a distractor. It's useful to remember that smells are particularly evocative, so scented things, like lavender bags or aromatic wooden objects, can be very distracting.

Exercise

Before going on to the next grounding technique, think what you might use as your grounding objects. Make a list.

Developing a "Grounding" Image

This is a visual picture which can soothe and distract you from a flashback or a nightmare: a safe place in your mind where you can go whenever you need to be calmed. Spend time thinking about the characteristics of your soothing, safe place. Do you want it to be public, like a busy ski slope or park, or private, like your own luxury home or secluded garden? Then make it interactive: if you choose a garden, know the layout so that you can walk around it and smell certain flowers, hear fountains in another section. If you enjoy feeling the sun on your shoulders then make it a warm day. You might imagine being involved in a hobby: try to get immersed in each stage of your painting, or piano playing, or grooming your horse. If you choose an image of a luxury home, walk from room to room, filling it with pleasing objects. Alternatively, you could choose to have a massage or beauty treatment in your imagination, if this would soothe you; again, plan the experience systematically.

All this planning is worth the effort because you will find that the image is so much more absorbing if it is pleasurable and detailed, and if you are familiar with the "route" that you take through it. Try to make it more vivid by physically or mentally collecting pictures or details for your "safe place" whenever you see advertisements, etc. The most important thing is that you should want to go to this place.

As with all the grounding techniques, you really must rehearse the image if it is going to be vivid and accessible enough for you to tune into when you have a flashback. With good planning, you will have chosen something that is so pleasing that it is not a chore to bring it to mind several times a day. The more you rehearse your positive image when you are feeling relaxed, the more easily you will be able to switch to it during an emotional crisis.

Finally, an extra useful aspect of your image is what I call a "bridging" image. Sometimes, you might have a flashback and need a link to get you to your "safe place." There are many images that you can use to help you make this link: for example, you might imagine yourself floating away from the traumatic scene and into your "safe place," or you might imagine a trusted friend taking you from one place to the other; you might imagine a wall crumbling to allow you out into a peaceful scene.

Exercise

- Start to work on your grounding image as soon as possible. It can be a powerful means of distraction.
- Try to make your image more vivid by sketching it, collecting magazine pictures of it and so on: the more vivid your image, the more distracting it will be.
- As with all the other techniques, practice will make you more skilled and this means that you will be more able to access the coping strategy when you are really upset.

Developing a "Grounding" Phrase

A ground phrase is a few words (or a tune) which are affirming and a reminder that you are surviving in the present. Phrases can range from a brief "I am OK" to lengthy statements like: "I have survived, I am strong, I believe in me and I will go on surviving." You can leave reminders of your affirming phrase around the house or in the car or on the computer screen, so that you get used to thinking it and can recall it when you need to ground yourself. If music is more grounding and soothing, try that.

Finding a "Grounding" Position

It's not uncommon for us to take on a bodily position which reflects our current thoughts and feelings, so bad memories can influence your posture and can echo the fear or hurt that you are feeling. The position of our bodies has been shown to influence the way we feel: for example, a "military" position tends to make us feel stronger. A "grounding position" is a physical position in which you feel safe and/or strong. Some find that curling up is comforting, while others might adopt a more upright stance with shoulders back. You need to discover what works for you, and then practice using this position whenever you can so that you can easily move into it and combat your distress.

Exercise

- Try out several positions until you find one or two that reliably leave you feeling safe or strong, or whatever it is that you need to feel.
- When you have discovered what works for you, keep adopting that position so that it becomes familiar and easy to turn to.

General Guidelines for Using Grounding Techniques

Although the principle of grounding is simple, its success requires personalization and practice. Personalization means that you need to find grounding techniques that really suit *you*. This can call for a lot of trial and error as you explore different options. Don't give up after trying just one or two ideas – it is worth investing time in finding the right technique. Once you have found strategies that suit you, you will need to practice (and practice). Distracting oneself from a bad memory or a flashback is difficult, and sometimes you won't manage it, but you will stand a better chance if you are so familiar with your grounding strategies that they are easily "switched on." The only way to achieve this is by practicing the strategies.

So, through the use of well rehearsed words, images and body positions, you can begin to take control over painful memories and flashbacks. For some, the control gained over the intrusive memories and flashbacks actually stops them from being such a problem. As confidence in managing them increases, their intensity can decrease. However, for others, grounding can provide only temporary relief and, if you find that the memories and flashbacks continue to give you unmanageable distress, then a different approach can be more helpful. Rather than trying to distract from the memory, this second approach requires you to face it. This can present a daunting prospect, so you need to consider whether you are prepared to remember. Read through the next section thoroughly before you decide whether or not to face your traumatic memories.

Choosing to Remember

None of us likes to remember painful memories, but, in order to recover from the effects of abuse, you might find it necessary to address what happened. This is an optional suggestion and you should never force yourself to review painful histories before you are ready. As we have already said, you can do a great deal of the work of recovery by using Part Two of this book alone, and not yet delving into the deeper issues of abuse tackled in Part Three.

We all recognize that recalling distressing memories is a difficult task, perhaps made more difficult by a concern that recollections might be "false memories." The reliability of memory has been studied by psychologists for many years and we do know that, for each of us, memory is fallible to some degree. However, as we discovered in Part One, memories are largely accurate and, although our recollections can be in error, this is more likely to reflect *inaccuracies* and not *false* memory.

Some memories haunt us because they have not been "laid to rest": they have not been emotionally processed, and so the impact of them remains very immediate. The aim of focusing on remembering the past is to achieve this emotional processing so that you can relegate memories to the past. This doesn't mean that the memories will stop being shocking or painful when you do review them, but that the memories won't be so prominent in your consciousness.

We fail to process memories emotionally when we avoid reflecting on the whole content of an experience with regard to our thoughts and feelings and what the event meant to us. It is very natural to avoid dwelling on that which frightens or hurts us, but avoidance invariably leads to the frightening or hurtful memories remaining vivid, sometimes in the form of intrusive memories and sometimes in the form of flashbacks (see Figure 11.1).

Figure 11.1:   **How Painful Memories Stay With Us**

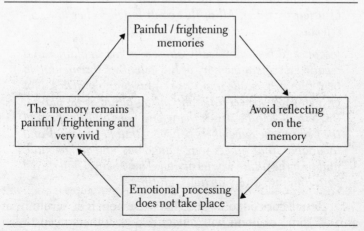

By recalling what has happened to you and dwelling more on the experience, you can begin the task of emotional processing, and this will help you to adjust to the memory and put it in the past. For some, there will be a single incident to be dealt with; for others there will be a series of memories which will need to be addressed.

An American psychologist, Dr P. Resick, has spent many years helping victims of sexual assault manage their traumatic memories. The advice she has for survivors of sexual trauma is equally relevant to all survivors of trauma. She suggests that, in remembering the past, you need to consider:

- what actually happened, in detail
- what you *felt* and *thought* during the traumatic experience
- what it *meant* to you. Ask yourself: "What did it lead me to believe about myself, about others and the future?"

For example:

Laurie was bullied at school and she recalled a playground experience of being humiliated by a group of children that she trusted. For her this meant that she was socially unacceptable, that she could not trust others and that she would always be a loner, never really being accepted by anyone. When she now remembered the incident, she not only felt the shame and hurt of the humiliation, but the meaning of it felt true, too. All of this contributed to her low self-esteem.

Joseph had been physically abused by his stepfather and recalled a typical memory of his stepfather threatening to beat him if he made a mistake in his piano practice. Not only did Joseph recall the mounting panic as he played, the terror when he struck the wrong note and the pain of the beating, he remembers believing that he was weak and incapable, that others were dangerous and judgmental, and that the future was terrifying. These beliefs had stayed with him into a very anxious adulthood.

Dr Resick goes on to suggest that these beliefs be scrutinized as only some of them will reflect reality. Others need to be reviewed so that a more balanced perspective can be achieved. For Laurie, a more balanced and accurate conclusion was that, although she had not fitted into her peer group at school, she was now quite socially able and had every chance of fitting in with adult groups. For Joseph, the balanced picture was that, as an adult, he had proved himself to be quite able and, although some people might not wish him well, most wouldn't hurt him, so there was no need to be afraid all of the time. Reaching these balanced conclusions requires some skill, but it is an important stage in processing the memory and placing it in the past. In Chapter 13, "Getting a Balanced Perspective," we will go through the steps involved in reviewing the conclusions that we draw from our experiences, but for the time being, simply focus on remembering.

You should not put yourself under pressure to do the next exercise too soon. Only begin recalling the past in detail *if you feel ready*. Some people prefer to do this part of the work with the support of a counsellor or therapist, and you could consider that option.

Exercise

If you feel that you are ready to review your past, you can make it easier by doing this in stages.

- If it is too difficult to write down a detailed emotional account straight away, start by writing what happened in a detached manner, rather like a police report – just bare facts.
- When you are able, rewrite your experiences but with as much detail as you can: sounds, smells, sights, sensations.
- Ultimately, you are aiming to write a vivid account which will not only recall what happened, but also what you felt and what went through your mind, including as much detail as you are able.

continued on next page

- If you can't recall details, it is better not to force yourself to remember things, just accept what you do remember.
- You might feel that you need to stop writing and so you should take a break, but try to continue with the account when you can.
- It is advisable to have a reasonable command of grounding skills and coping strategies, so that you can care for yourself if you get distressed. If it helps, use the support of a trusted partner or friend.
- When you have a final account, reread it with compassion for yourself. Feel as much emotion as you can, but don't judge yourself: try to feel as protective towards yourself, as you would towards any child. By rereading the account you will be continuing the task of emotional processing.
- If you can, work out the *meaning* of your experience so that you can review this later.

Key Points

- One way of managing problem memories is to avoid the things that trigger them, at least while you are developing the ability to take command of them.
- You can use grounding strategies to "switch off" the traumatic memories, although this requires a great deal of practice.
- Sometimes, the only way of managing the memories is to "face" them, to review in detail what happened to you and what it meant to you. This allows you to "process" the memories in a way which enable you to then relegate them to the past.

12

Working on Your Self-Image and Self-Protection

Improving Your Self-Image

Although some survivors of abuse have a very clear sense of self-worth, others struggle with poor self-image, or low self-esteem, and this can be a significant handicap to recovery. As we saw in Part One, early experiences of abuse affect a person's view of her- or himself and tend to damage their self-concept. In coming to understand more about your difficulties, you may already have identified low self-esteem as one of your problems.

If you were abused as a child, you may have been denied the opportunity to learn that you were precious, that you deserved love, that you were special and that you were OK just the way you were. You may not have been given the chance to feel good about yourself. Some of you may have had one or more important figures who valued you, and enabled you to develop a sense of being worthwhile. Some of you will have had no one.

Whenever you go through the process of remembering what happened to you, feelings which fuel low self-esteem, such as shame and worthlessness, may be stirred up even further. In order to heal it is important to learn how to feel worthwhile, and how to value yourself. So, in this section, we will be looking at ways of building up your self-esteem.

This section might look rather like a list of "top tips" to work through, and indeed, it is a good idea to be systematic in your approach; however, self-esteem is only built over weeks and months, so this is just a starting place where you can begin the task of slowly but surely building a more positive sense of yourself.

Exercise

- As a first step, you might consider what you value in others. Try not to think of yourself: instead, think of friends, family members or colleagues with whom you would like to spend time. Reflect on the personal qualities which make them enjoyable company – for example: they are good listeners; they are always helpful; they are kind, or genuine, or smile readily. You might discover that you value qualities such as openness, honesty, humor, concern, reliability, sincerity and so on. List these sorts of attributes and make your list as long as you can.

- When you have made your list, look back over it and note how many of the qualities on the list could also apply to you. You might well find it difficult to recognize these positive qualities – that's part of the problem of low self-esteem – so try to stand outside yourself and consider which of these qualities a friend would say that you had. If you are able, it might be worth actually asking an honest friend for their opinion. I can't emphasize enough just how important it is to recognize your good qualities.

In addition to pinpointing good qualities as outlined in this exercise, there are a number of practical ways in which you can enhance your self-image.

Find Pleasurable Activities

What do you like to do? With whom do you like to spend time? What do you find worthwhile? Make a list of these pleasurable activities. Remember, you do have to make pleasurable activities a priority. If you are not used to doing things that are pleasing for you, you might well need to make "formal" arrangements and actually schedule pleasant events in your diary, however small the occasion. If you are feeling depressed, it can be especially difficult to find enjoyment in things, so try to recall what *used* to give you pleasure and use this as a starting point.

Always look for opportunities to identify and accentuate the positives in yourself and do things which are important to you. Think about the positive changes that you would like to make in your life and list things that you can do to get the process started. It is all too easy to forget resolutions to make something happen, so identify a realistic review date for yourself when you will look back and evaluate how far you have succeeded in putting your plans into action.

Find People You Like

An important route to creating a good self-image is making efforts to be with those who make you feel good: those who view you positively, who believe in your strengths, your worth, your capacity to manage your own life. It's a good idea to structure your life so that you are in contact with others who respect you, understand you and take you seriously. Make a note of those with whom you feel good and try to spend more time with them. Similarly, note those who leave you feeling bad about yourself and make efforts not to be with them.

Nurture Yourself

Identify personal experiences that make you feel good – taking bubble baths, buying flowers, going for a swim – and do them often. This is an essential part of feeling good about yourself. Once a day, at least, do something nice for yourself. This might feel uncomfortable at first but, as with most things, it will get easier with practice. If you are used to neglecting yourself, you could easily forget to fit in times when you nurture yourself, so schedule them in your diary, and/or make a commitment to do something pleasurable with a friend, so that you are more likely to make the effort.

Keep a Record of the Positive Things in Your Life

Make an extra effort not to discount your positive experiences and achievements, however minor they might seem. These might include: finishing a task, recalling something pleasant from the past, receiving compliments. These constant reminders, however small, will build up over time and will help you develop a more positive view of yourself, but in order to create this list you must be vigilant.

It is easy to minimize, ignore or forget successes if you are not practiced at recognizing them. Remember how effectively negative belief systems fuel negative thinking, and how often you dismiss a compliment or downgrade your achievements. Even if you don't actively rubbish the good experience, how often do you simply forget? It's as if there's no "pigeon hole" in your memory banks for the good stuff.

Another suggestion from Dr Padesky is to keep a written log of the good things that happen to you. This *"Positive" Record* will help you hold on to the important information about yourself. There is an example of one below in Table 12.1. The more positive events and qualities you can recall, the more you will build your self-image and the more easily you will be able to challenge a negative view of yourself. Eventually this will help you to weaken your negative beliefs and establish more helpful ones.

Table 12.1:	"Positive" Record
Date	**Good things about me**
2.4.99	I helped Sara start her car this morning: this shows that I'm a good friend and I'm quite clever with cars. Julie said that I make her laugh more than anyone else she knows: this shows that I have a sense of humor and I'm entertaining.
3.4.99	I finished a huge project at work today. This took a lot of effort on my part and it shows that I am capable and hardworking.
6.4.99	I completed my tax form on time this year! This was much more of an effort than finishing the project – I did well!
9.4.99	.... and so on
	WEEKLY SUMMING UP I've seen that I can be sociable and thoughtful as well as being hardworking and organized . . . and . . . I feel embarrassed writing this, so I'm not big-headed!

This log is important, so consider dedicating part of your note-book to it – you might even get a separate book for this purpose. As it is often difficult to remember achievements and compliments, make sure that you have ready access to your log so that you can write the positives down before you forget them! This might mean carrying your notebook around with you, so find a portable one or dedicate a few pages of your personal organizer to this.

As with all record-keeping, this might seem like a chore, but it will pay off. This particular task gets easier with time: the more positives you appreciate, the better your self-esteem and the more sensitive you will be to achievements. A positive cycle, for a change. Gradually, you will be able to "tune into" the positives more easily. At times, however, it will be difficult to recognize them, particularly when you are tired, stressed or unwell. At those times, ask someone close to you to help out.

Exercise

- Start keeping a log a soon as possible.
- Once you have entries in your log, you must reread them if they are going to have an impact on the way you see yourself. Try to do this regularly, say every week, and try to sum up what you have learnt about yourself in that time. This will help to reinforce your new self-image.

Re-Appraising Your Self-Image

It is only fair to acknowledge that building a positive image is challenging, especially in the early days of recovery, and you can expect to have ups and downs. Remember how old beliefs can "fight for survival"? By doing these exercises, you will begin to appreciate your good qualities and you will be more easily able to look at and change your negative self-image when you get to Chapter 13, "Getting a Balanced Perspective."

If you can, use others to help you re-evaluate yourself. A friend's view can help, even if it's hard to believe. Always listen to the good things that friends have to say about you, and note the positive view that others have of you. Over time, you can use this sort of feedback, and your own observations, to build up your positive self-image. Difficult as it may be, try to put down a new description of yourself, based on what you learn. Over the course of this book, you might well want to add to this description.

Not all self-esteem boosting activities have to be planned so well in advance. If you are feeling very negative about yourself, think of some manageable task that you can handle, *now*. A sense of accomplishment, however small, can help to restore feelings of self-worth.

Looking After Yourself: Combating the Urges to Self-Harm

Some survivors of abuse have suicidal feelings or the urge to harm themselves at some time in their life. This is not unusual, and it is certainly not crazy. Having such feelings is very different from acting upon them, and acknowledging them is not an inevitable step towards harming yourself. So, don't be afraid to recognize your feelings. Instead, try to understand why you have the urge to hurt yourself.

Self-Injury

In the last several years, there has been more media reporting of "self-injury," "self-harm" or self-mutilation" than before; it is not as taboo a subject as it used to be. These terms refer to self-inflicted hurt, such as cutting or burning oneself, a practice that is not as rare as we might like to think.

Those of you who do injure yourself in some way will be only too familiar with the forms it can take, so I won't elaborate on these here. Rather, I'd like to emphasize how important it is to discover what drives the behavior, as this is the first step towards taking control over it.

The urge to injure oneself often makes sense when one considers the immediate effect of it. The initial response is often relief from tension or distraction from worse pain. Physical harm to the body causes actual changes in our brain chemistry, and in this way can make us feel numb or even elated. These feelings of numbness or elation are often preferable to feeling the emotional pain that many survivors struggle with, so it's no wonder that some turn to self-harm.

To a very minor extent, we all experience this: the tense person who bangs his fist on the table and gains a sense of release, or the person undergoing unpleasant dental treatment who clenches her fist really hard in order to divert her attention away from the pain in her mouth. Tension release and distraction are two of the most common explanations for self-injury and, at least in the short term, it is effective.

Like many of the difficulties that we've discussed, a natural inclination to divert ourselves from pain can present a real problem when the impulse becomes exaggerated, when the distraction becomes extreme. Some people find themselves using self-harm frequently, often resorting to increasingly severe forms of self-inflicted injury. Many describe a reliance on self-harm that sounds very similar to addiction, with powerful urges and cravings. It's not surprising, therefore, that some find it very difficult to give up self-harm once they have discovered it.

Sometimes self-injury is less obvious and takes the form of drug and alcohol misuse or an eating disorder. Again, this can usually be understood as a coping strategy gone wrong. Among those who misuse drugs, alcohol and food, many recognize that they can numb, or even forget, painful memories and feelings in this way. Self-neglect is another subtle form of self-harm: not caring about diet and health is sometimes a way of playing Russian Roulette with a life.

If you are injuring yourself, please seek professional support. It isn't easy to break out of the addiction to self-harm without support and, as long as you hurt yourself, you are in physical danger. Your GP or a good therapist is likely to be familiar with this form of coping and you will probably find they are understanding rather than shocked. If you find that your GP is not responsive, don't give up on the profession; instead, try to see a different doctor.

Occasionally, the drive to harm oneself goes yet further and a person can have thoughts of suicide. Again, having suicidal thoughts doesn't mean that they will be acted on, but sometimes, when one feels completely hopeless, suicide seems the only way out. If you find that you are thinking of killing yourself, you should certainly seek help. Contact a support agency like Samaritans, Befrienders International or United Way when you feel in crisis, and when you can, see your GP. At the very least, if you have friends you can trust, talk to them about your feelings.

Research has shown that people harm themselves when it seems like the best option at the time. So, in principle, if there are other options these can offer alternative ways of coping. However, it is almost impossible to come up with other options when one is struggling with a powerful urge to self-harm and, because of this, it is crucial to have worked out a plan in advance. The aim of the plan is to help you cope and to get relief from your distress in a way which will not damage you.

Curbing the Urge to Harm Yourself: Devising a Plan

When you are not feeling so desperate that it's hard to think clearly, consider the following:

- If you have felt suicidal or you have had strong urges to self-harm in the past, try to identify what sets off this feeling so that you can know when you are most vulnerable. Write down the things that trigger your urges to self-harm: if you know them, you can anticipate them. Once you know when you are vulnerable, you can begin to plan to avoid those situations which put you most at risk. If the urges to self-harm feel pretty constant, try to identify when the urges increase or decrease, even slightly. You can then, at least, try to avoid those things which worsen the urges.

- Look back at the "Coping Strategies" list you compiled when working through Chapter 10 and see how many of these you can use in order to curb the urges. Bear in mind that the coping strategies that you choose will be most effective if they achieve the same ends as the self-harm. For example, if self-harm helps you to achieve a peaceful, relaxed state, then using relaxation exercises will be helpful; if self-harm acts as a distraction technique, use your grounding strategies; if self-harm gives you a sense of being real, try to find a non-harmful way of achieving this. It is only fair to recognize that self-harm is powerful and usually has immediate and dramatic effect, and your substitute coping strategy will probably not be able to give you the same effect. What you can anticipate is that your substitute strategy will take the edge off the urge so that you can resist it more easily.

- Make a contract with someone, or more than one person, not to kill or harm yourself. Try to use someone who matters to you, as this will help you to keep the contract. This might be a family member, a friend or your doctor.

- Instead of harming yourself, phone for help when you feel at your worst. Have a *list* of important telephone numbers ready to hand. The list can contain the numbers of both friends and professionals. Check out the public helplines in your area. When you are feeling at your worst, you won't be able to call this list to mind very easily, so keep it somewhere accessible. Put it on a sticky label on the telephone, if necessary.

- If it is possible, avoid having the means of killing or harming yourself close at hand, as this often makes it easier to give in to the urges. For example, don't keep pills and razor blades in the house, if you can manage without them.

- Write down the reasons why you should live and not harm yourself. Keep this reminder ready to hand, perhaps on an index card that you can carry around. Your reasons might include: *I did nothing wrong, I don't deserve to hurt myself; he's not going to beat me; my children love me and I love them.* If you have difficulty coming up with reasons, ask someone close to help you. This will be an important statement. Keep it somewhere safe and accessible.

Exercise

- If you self-harm, make sure that you find time to address the six points above.
- Write notes so that you can remind yourself of key messages when you are feeling vulnerable, and make sure that you always have access to your notes.

Key Points

- You can improve your self-image by finding pleasurable activities, mixing with people that value you and by learning to nurture yourself.
- It can be easy to forget one's strengths and positive qualities, so keeping a concrete record of achievements and compliments (however small) can help you keep a positive view of yourself in mind.
- Very low self-esteem and distress can result in self-injury. There are steps that can be taken to combat this. If you are at risk, it is crucial that you take these steps.

13

Getting a
Balanced Perspective

By now, it will be clear that the way we think influences the way we feel. If I see a bus coming towards me and think: "It's going to hit me!", then I feel fear; if I see a friend coming towards me and think: "She's going to greet me – how nice!", then I feel pleasure. If my automatic thoughts are accurate, the feelings that I get can help me prepare myself: the fear makes me get out of the way of the bus and the feelings of pleasure mean that I'm friendly and welcoming towards my friend.

But suppose I misjudged what I saw and the bus wasn't heading for me, or the friend was actually very hostile. Then my misreading of the situation would have caused me unnecessary fear in the first instance and, worse still, would have prevented me from protecting myself against my so-called friend, in the second. We all misjudge situations from time to time but, if we do it too much, we can find that it causes us problems such as unnecessary misery or worry.

For some time, you have been noting your feelings and linking them with what's happening around you and what runs through your mind. Now you can take this a step further and learn to review your automatic thoughts, looking for misjudgments. If you can pinpoint these, then you can work on them to gain a more balanced perspective. Reviewing thoughts in this way is made easier if you are first aware of the range of common misjudgments that we can make.

Misjudgments

In Part One, we saw that extreme belief systems (some of which are actually more like prejudices) affect our perceptions so that we tend to see things in a way that fits with our beliefs. There is no problem if the belief system is realistic, in which case we are likely to judge things accurately; but if the belief system is incorrect, we still tend to bias our judgements to fit. We "skew" our thinking in accordance with our incorrect belief system: hence the misjudgment.

Each of us is prone to "skewed thinking," from time to time. We tend to be particularly vulnerable at times of high stress or low mood, or even when we are feeling overconfident. When we are stressed we are more likely to view things in an alarming way; when our mood is low, our biases tend to be pessimistic; and when we are overconfident, we view things far too positively.

Two classic examples of anxiety triggering alarming misjudgments are the nervous student who *over*estimates the likelihood of failing an exam, and the nervous traveller who *over*estimates the chance of a plane crash. When we are down, however, the most common misjudgment is to see the future as more hopeless than it really is. In contrast, when we are overconfident we overestimate what we can achieve and this sometimes results in disappointment. Although such thinking biases are quite normal in certain situations, problems arise when we keep making misjudgments.

Below is a list of the most common biases in thinking. The list is long because misjudgments are common.

Exercise

- Read slowly through the list of common types of misjudgment and consider which you are most prone to.
- It is important that you get to know how *you* tend to misjudge situations, so that you can be on the lookout for biases in your thinking.

Common misjudgments	What it means
ALL-OR-NOTHING THINKING	Seeing things in black and white categories, missing the "grey" areas. Things are good *or* bad, successes *or* failures (and the tendency is to see the "bad" and the "failure" more easily).

Examples: *Nothing is ever going to go right for me. I can trust no one. I am a total failure.*

CATASTROPHIZATION	Predicting the *very* worst, sometimes from a very benign starting point. This often happens very rapidly, so that before we know it, we are holding a really alarming thought or image.

Examples: *I made a mistake, my boss will be furious, my contract won't be renewed, I'm going to lose my job. I disagreed with Jane, she probably hates me now, she won't want anything more to do with me, I'm going to be so lonely.*

OVERGENERALIZATION	Seeing a negative event as an indication of *everything* being negative, *always*.

Examples: *I've failed an interview – I'll never get a job. This relationship is going badly – I'll never find a partner. She let me down – I can trust no one.*

USING A "MENTAL FILTER"	Picking out a single (negative) feature and dwelling on it without reference to other (good) things which might have happened. Focusing on the one thing that you didn't do well today, while forgetting your achievements or picking up an

a single criticism about your work or your appearance, forgetting all the compliments that you have received

Examples: *One of my exam marks is low – this is terrible – I'm really no good at this job.*

DISQUALIFYING THE POSITIVE

Recognizing something good in yourself or your life and rejecting it, downgrading it or dismissing it as unimportant.

Examples: *He's only saying that to be nice. She's probably trying to get something from me. Well, this was only a small achievement – other people do better.*

Both disqualifying the positive and using a mental filter are closely linked with:

MAGNIFICATION/ MINIMIZATION

Exaggerating the importance of negative events and underestimating the importance of positive events.

Example: *I can't stop thinking about the mess-up I made at work today. I know that I managed to get the deal through, but I didn't handle it well.*

JUMPING TO CONCLUSIONS

Making interpretations in the absence of facts to support your conclusion. This falls into two categories: MIND READING and FORTUNE TELLING.

Examples: MIND READING: *I just know that he was thinking badly of me; I know that they were all laughing at me.* FORTUNE TELLING: *It's going to be a terrible day; I'm going to fail this interview. When I meet him, he's going to dislike me.*

Jumping to conclusions is often linked with:

EMOTIONAL REASONING	Assuming that what you *feel* is bad must *be* bad. Just because something *feels* as though it is happening, or will happen, that doesn't make it real. Ancient man *felt* that the world was flat but it isn't!

Examples: *I feel as though I'm going to pass out, so I will collapse. I feel awful when I get angry, therefore it's bad to get angry. I feel as though I am a bad person, therefore I must be a bad person.*

TAKING THINGS PERSONALLY	Assuming that, if something bad or threatening happens, it's directed at you. If someone leaves your lecture it's because they are bored or dislike you, rather than because they are rude or perhaps need the bathroom.

Example: *Sue's dinner party didn't go well; I'm sure it was because I was feeling awkward and made everyone else feel uncomfortable.*

SELF-BLAME OR CRITICISM	Seeing yourself as the cause of a bad event for which you were not responsible or criticizing yourself for things that are not really your fault.

Examples: *I feel ill, I must have brought it on myself. I can't catch up with my work – it's because I'm stupid and lazy.*

NAME-CALLING	Calling yourself names that you probably would never attach to a friend, being far too harsh on yourself. It's not character-build-

ing to be hard on yourself and it very likely keeps your self-esteem low.

Examples: *Idiot! I am so stupid! What a fool I am!*

UNREALISTIC EXPECTATIONS — Using exaggerated performance criteria for yourself and others. Using "shoulds" and "oughts" and "musts" in your expectations of yourself and, sometimes, your demands of others.

Examples: *Unless it's the best it doesn't count. I should get full marks. I shouldn't make a mistake. I must get everything right. I must please everyone.*

Unless our biased thinking is skewed towards the positive, misjudgments or biases tend to increase our distress and can leave us feeling worse than ever, as shown in Figure 13.1.

Figure 13.1: **The Misjudgment–Distress Cycle**

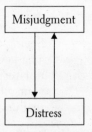

For example, if a man always viewed relationships in an "all-or-nothing" way, his interpretation of a minor row is likely to be: "That's it! The relationship is over!" Understandably, this would cause him great upset and, in turn, his high levels of distress would affect his perceptions and fuel more thinking biases. He might begin to conclude (incorrectly):

"Relationships always go wrong for me" (overgeneralization)

"I am completely hopeless and unlovable" (disqualifying the positive)

"I will never be able to have a decent relationship and I'll live out my life lonely and unloved!" (catastrophizing)

One thinking bias leads to another and he is going to feel worse than ever.

You can see that it is important for all of us to be aware of the accuracy of our automatic thoughts and conclusions. If our thinking is negatively biased, we will draw conclusions that are just not fair on us. The diaries that you have been keeping might help you spot some of your typical biases. When you identify one of these classic thinking biases, try to recall how this affected the way you felt, your view of yourself and your subsequent behavior. Did they cause problems for you? At the end of this chapter is another form of the diary (Diary 2: Analyzing biased thinking) which is designed to help you tease out the thinking biases and, when you're ready, come up with an alternative, more balanced way of viewing things. You will find more of these forms in the appendix.

Thinking biases can occur when we contemplate either the present or the past. For example, a woman who was subjected to a great deal of abuse from her parents might recall the pain of this but might no longer remember the praise which they sometimes gave her. Without the ability to recollect her parents' good opinion of her, she might feel totally demoralized and of little worth (a retrospective negative bias). As an adult with a low opinion of herself, she could easily continue to be skewed towards the negative and be insensitive to praise and compliments (a negative bias in the present). If she maintains a biased perspective she can only draw conclusions which are distressing. This will mean that she will hold on to a demoralized sense of herself and won't be able to build up a feeling of self-worth.

Reviewing "All-Or-Nothing" Thinking

One type of misjudgment, in particular, seems to be very common among the clients we meet in our clinic: "all-or-nothing thinking". This tendency to see only the extremes prevents us from recognizing the true range of possibilities. Typical extremes that we see are:

- *success or failure*, rather than degrees of success
- *thin or fat*, rather than a range of body shapes and weights
- *love or hatred*, rather than fluctuating emotion, or degrees of feeling
- *good or bad*, rather than a whole spectrum of worth

There is a tendency not only to categorize in this way, but also to find only one of the extremes acceptable. Most, although not all, of our clients are only satisfied with "success" or "thin" or "love" or "good" – very high expectations, indeed.

This "all-or-nothing" thinking can be applied to oneself, but also to others and to situations. Some examples of this are shown in Table 13.1.

Table 13.1:	All-or-Nothing Thinking	
Self	Others	Situations
I made a mistake, therefore I'm a failure. I broke my diet: I'm a failure and I'm fat.	Steven doesn't smile at me: he must hate me. She misled me: she's a nasty piece of work. She misled me: she is totally untrustworthy.	The bus didn't turn up: you can't rely on anything in this town. It's raining on my day off: life is awful.

Although this extreme thinking style often poses problems, "all-or-nothing thinking" can seem to have advantages. For example, we can feel as though we have fewer dilemmas to deal with: things are right *or* wrong, black *or* white, so decision-making is less complicated. If we begin to consider that there are degrees of right and wrong, that there might be "grey" areas, decision-making becomes more complicated and can feel more risky.

Despite its apparent advantages, we must often conclude that "all-or-nothing" thinking is not in our best interest. Take the statement: "If I assume that I can trust no one, I will not get hurt." The apparent advantage of this extreme position is that a person holding it might feel safe from being hurt by another, but the disadvantage of this view is that this person will be very lonely. Alternatively, consider the statement: "Either I succeed (completely) or I have failed." The apparent advantage here is that this reasoning might drive a person on, give her the incentive to aim high; but the disadvantage is that there is always a high chance of not succeeding and so frequent "failure" is inevitable.

Exercise

- Reflect on the areas of your life or the personal qualities which you see in extreme terms. Look back through your diaries for examples.
- What are your pros and cons of seeing things as all or nothing?

The disadvantages of holding an "all-or-nothing" view are increased if a person tends to bias his conclusions so that disappointment is more likely than satisfaction. The "complete success" or "failure" extreme is a good example of this. Another common extreme involves trust: unless someone is "100 per cent trustworthy" they are put in a "totally untrustworthy" category. Such high expectations of others are almost certainly going to result in disappointments.

Therefore, it can be useful to develop the habit of reviewing extreme thinking by asking yourself: "Is this really all or nothing . . ."

❏   ❏
Success   *or*   Failure

❏   ❏
Trustworthiness   *or*   Untrustworthiness

. . . or are there areas which I am not noticing?"

❏ .... ❏
Success/Near total success/Partial success/Perhaps not great/Partial failure/Failure

❏ .... ❏
Totally trustworthy/Mostly trustworthy/Trustworthy with minor things/Untrustworthy

---

Exercise

What aspects of yourself, others or situations do you tend
to view as "all or nothing"?
• First list those areas where you tend to adopt an all-or-
  nothing position.
• Then try to identify the "grey" areas.

1 ❏ .... ❏

   ....

2 ❏ .... ❏

   ....

3 ❏ .... ❏

   ....

4 ❏ .... ❏

   ....

It will take time and practice to develop the habit of looking
for the "grey" areas. You might find it difficult at first – try
not to regard this as a failure.

Reviewing Distressing Thoughts and Images

Once you have identified a distressing thought or image, you can review it and decide if it is accurate or skewed. If it is skewed, then you can work on it to develop a more balanced view.

This is a demanding task which requires quite a lot of practice. At first, you might not be able to see misjudgments very easily, but with time you will find them easier to spot. It's rather like the beginner birdwatcher or antique collector who at first cannot easily distinguish breeds of birds or tell fake antiques from real ones. Over time, each gets better at discriminating and each begins to be able to recognize subtle differences. Eventually, the birdwatcher can reliably identify breeds of bird and the antique collector grows confident about recognizing the real antiques. But this takes time and practice.

Working on your distressing thoughts is easier if you ask yourself the following six questions. They will help you get a wider perspective on the situation.

1 *"Just what are my upsetting thoughts or images?"*
    Be as precise as you can and use your diaries to help you.
2 *"Are there biases in my view of things?"*
    Try to stand back and look for distortions and exaggerations in your outlook.
3 *"Is there evidence to support my thought or image?"*
    Some of our upsetting thoughts are accurate, some are not and some have a grain of truth in them. What experience or knowledge do you have which fits with your distressing view of things?
4 *"What is the evidence that does not support my thought?"*
    The answer to this question will balance question 3. Try to review your experiences and list anything which you could use to argue against your original view. Think how someone else might view the situation. As this is the most difficult step, below is a list of questions that can help you review your automatic thoughts:

    • Am I missing something important? Have I looked at all the facts?

- Am I asking questions that have no answers?
- Have I had experiences that don't fit in with my upsetting thought?
- If someone else had this thought, what would I say to them?
- If I told my best friend about this thought, what would s/he say?
- When I'm feeling good in myself, how would I view the situation?

At this point, you can start to think about alternative ways of looking at the situation. If you feel up to it, there are a couple of useful questions that you could then ask yourself:

5 *"What is the worst thing that could happen?"*
   This can be frightening to consider, but addressing your worst fear will put you in a better position to tackle it.
6 *"How could I cope if the worst happened?"*
   Once you have faced your fear, start to problem solve. Ask others to help, if you can.

By answering these six questions, you have given yourself a wider perspective:

- you have considered the evidence for and against your negative thought;
- you have considered how you would cope with the worst outcome.

Now, you are in a good position to challenge your negative thought and substitute a new, balanced appraisal of yourself or your situation.

The purpose of reappraising your upsetting thoughts is not to find some comforting platitude or glib statement. The aim is to come up with a genuine, balanced statement.

Testing Out a New View: Taking Action

Whenever it is possible, test out your new appraisal as this will help you to assure yourself of your new view of things. Most of us don't believe things without some evidence, and that's what you will be gathering. Actually testing out your new view will demonstrate that you are not simply saying soothing nothings to yourself.

So ask yourself: "How can I check out my new conclusion? What can I do to see if I'm right?" You might find that you consult others' opinions; you might adopt a new way of coping; you might stop avoiding something; you might behave differently with people. This list could be endless, but whatever you do, you will very likely find that you face the prospect of doing things differently from usual. So you could find that testing things out is risky and challenging, and you might be tempted to skip it.

Not testing out your new view means that you won't gather the evidence that could help you believe in a new perspective. If a new workmate arrived boasting that he was excellent at the job, you might give him the benefit of the doubt for a while, but if he didn't actually prove himself, you would soon doubt his claims. In the same way, you might be comforted by a reassuring reappraisal of a distressing thought, but unless this gets backed up by action, you will soon lose faith in it.

Below are the examples of Mary and Martin, who first review their distressing thoughts, and then work out an action plan to check out their new, balanced perspective.

Mary: "I'm a lousy mother."

1 Negative thought: *"The children are quarrelling again – I'm a lousy mother."*
2 Thinking biases: Self-blame; overgeneralization; unrealistic expectations.
3 Support for thought: *"They are fighting with each other and I can't stop them."*
4 Evidence against thought: *"All children fight at some time. My children are just normal kids and one fight doesn't make me a bad mother. I can probably think of reasons why I am a good mother when I'm not feeling so low."*
5 Worst thing: *"That the children won't stop fighting and I won't be able to separate them."*

6 Coping: "*I could ring their father, who would come home in his lunch break and give me a hand in dealing with this situation. I don't have to manage on my own.*"

Balanced restatement: "*My children are fighting, just like kids do. This does not make me a bad mother, but it does get me down when I'm low. Even if they continued to fight, there's a solution because their father could come home and settle them.*"

Action: "*I can check out whether or not I am a bad mother by phoning some friends with children and finding out what they think.*"

Martin: "I've lost a friend."

1 Negative thought: "*Paul was really 'off' with me at work. He's never liked me. That's someone else that I don't get along with.*"
2 Thinking biases: All or nothing; overgeneralization.
3 Support for thought: "*This has happened before.*"
4 Evidence against thought: "*He hasn't been 'off' with me before and I can't think of anything that I could have done to offend him. There are several workers in the office that are civil to me.*"
5 Worst thing: "*That I'm right and I end up without a friend in the world.*"
6 Coping: "*I could give people a second chance and try harder to mend bridges.*"

Balanced restatement: "*Paul was 'off' with me today- I don't know why. Perhaps he has a problem that he's dealing with. Even if Paul no longer wants to be friendly, there are others in the office who do. I can't please everyone all of the time and if I do fall out with someone I can take the initiative and try to repair the friendship.*"

Action: "*I can check out how Paul really feels by asking him if there's something wrong.*"

You will find more examples like this as you work through the book, so the steps in re-evaluating your distressing thoughts will get more and more familiar.

You can also use "Action Plans" to check out things about which you are unsure. For example, if you are unsure whether or not you can cope in a certain situation, or face something that worries you, or achieve a goal, then working out an action plan can help you establish your capabilities. The alternative is often avoiding that which worries us, and avoidance simply keeps our fears and uncertainties in place. You can use the six-question formula to help you to do this, as in the following example.

Richard: "I don't know if I can cope with the office party."

1 Negative thought: *"I'm completely anxious in social situations. I can't stand the tension and I make a mess of everything. I'd rather stay at home."*
2 Thinking biases: All or nothing; catastrophization.
3 Support for thought: *"I've been at parties and felt nervous and I've been a dead loss."*
4 Evidence against thought: *"I've been at parties and it's been OK. I've even enjoyed myself sometimes. If I stay at home, I also feel bad."*
5 Worst thing: *"That I'll be tense and clumsy and everyone will think me a fool."*
6 Coping: *"I could go to the party, but have an excuse if I feel uncomfortable and want to leave early. After all, no one can make me stay. I could make sure that I spend some time with Jim because I'm comfortable around him."*

Balanced restatement: *"I don't find some parties easy, but I also don't really want to stay at home. If I keep avoiding social events, I'll never get my confidence back and the only way to find out if I can cope is by going along. If I feel too uncomfortable, I don't have to stay."*

Action: *"I'll go to the party and I'll stay as long as I can; however, I'll rehearse an excuse just in case I need it. I'll also ring Jim – if he's going to the party, I'll find staying there even easier."*

Clearly, taking action means taking risks and, by definition, risks can mean disappointment. The two golden rules when you are risk-taking are:

- Minimize the risk: plan well ahead and work out the least risky strategy for you.
- Give yourself credit even when things go wrong, and learn from setbacks.

Eventually, you will be able to challenge biased thinking without having to write down each stage, but at first you will find it easier if you detail the thoughts, the biases and the challenges. This will help you develop a good technique and will ensure that you don't miss out important aspects of the challenging process. Use the recording diary sheet at the end of this chapter as a guide to challenging biased thinking.

Over time you will be able to abandon the lengthy recording sheet and substitute a shorter "aide memoire", a reminder of how to reappraise thoughts:

Upsetting thought: ....

I think like this because: ....

However: ....

Therefore: ....

Below are examples of this is action.

Mary
Upsetting thought: *I'm a lousy mother.*
I think like this because: *I blame myself very easily and I'm insecure.*
However: *I know this is normal kid's behavior.*
Therefore: *I'll ignore it for now and ring their dad if it gets out of hand. If I keep feeling unconfident, I'll ring a friend.*

Martin

Upsetting thought: *I've lost my friend.*

I think like this because: *I tend to look for the worst possibility and I'm not confident in myself.*

However: *Paul's probably having a bad day.*

Therefore: *I'll ask him how he is.*

Richard

Worrying thought: *I don't know if I can cope with the office party.*

I think like this because: *I've lost social confidence in myself.*

However: *I won't get my confidence back if I stay at home.*

Therefore: *I'll go and make my excuses to leave if necessary.*

It is crucial that you don't use the brief form of challenging before you've mastered the lengthy technique. That would be like trying to take a short cut before you know the lie of the land. The short cut just might work, but you could get lost and end up not knowing where to go next.

Exercise

Now it's time for you to begin to reappraise your distressing thoughts. Use Diary 2 at the end of this chapter and the list of six helpful questions above as a guide.

Key Points

- We all make misjudgments, but if this happens too frequently, it can cause us problems, like unnecessary misery or worry.
- We can learn to recognize misjudgments and correct them by systematically working through key questions.
- With practice, this process can become second nature.

Diary 2: Analyzing Biased Thinking

Monitor your feelings each day, noting when you feel particularly upset or particularly good. Jot down what went through your mind at the time. When you feel distressed, try to identify thinking biases and then see if you can challenge the upsetting thought. When you have worked out a challenging statement, re-rate your distress so that you can see the impact of your challenge. Rate your distress on the following scale:

1	2	3	4	5	6	7	8	9	10
No distress, calm				Moderate distress					As distressed as possible

Note these details as near to the time of the distress as you can – it is easy to forget later!

Date/time	What was going through my mind?	Distress rating	What were my thinking biases?	How would I view the situation now?	Re-rating

PART THREE

Working Through Key Issues

This final section of the book deals with some key issues for survivors of childhood trauma. This is not so much "what-to-do" as a "what-to-start-thinking-about" guide. You will not be learning so many techniques in Part Three, but you will be widening your perspectives.

The issues raised in this part of the book reflect the topics which have come up over and over again in our clinic, and the order in which they appear reflects the sequence which our clients told us was most comfortable for them.

Part Three begins with the issue of "blame" and moves on to dealing with anger because many clients told us that blame was a dominant issue and, as they began to shift their sense of self-blame, they grew angry. As we left blame and anger behind, the natural progress seemed to be opening up more about the experience of abuse and beginning to address its impact on relationships. Therefore, you'll find chapters on speaking out and confronting others, communicating with your family, dealing with intimacy and, finally, dealing with sexual difficulties. The next chapter addresses the losses that survivors feel when they appreciate the full impact of trauma on their childhood, their self-esteem and their relationships, and the final chapters focus on moving forward, looking after yourself from now on and continuing the work.

The purpose of each chapter is to help you to begin thinking about key issues and, if it's the right time for you, to start working through them. Most of the chapters have recommendations for further reading so, if the issue in that particular chapter is relevant to you, you can continue to tackle it using other self-help books. These issues can take a while to work through and resolve, and you might only start the work here.

14

Understanding Blame

It is natural for us to try to make sense of our world. In 1997, when Princess Diana was killed, nations asked, "Why?" and "How?" When we have an unusually rainy summer, we speculate: Is it because of global warming? . . . Is it linked to sun spots? . . . Is the climate changing? If we are hurt by someone, we also look for the reason. It is human to seek explanation.

If we don't have all the necessary information, however, we can draw the wrong conclusion. In the absence of information about the car crash in which Princess Diana died, many wild and incorrect theories began to abound – all driven by a natural impulse to understand. Now, when we have a rainy summer, meteorologists can give us a scientific explanation, but without this knowledge, primitive man believed that the gods were angry. If we don't have access to the complete picture, we make sense of things as best we can, and as a result we can draw very incorrect conclusions.

Children strive to understand why someone is hurting them and, without anyone to explain, they usually assume that they are to blame. Often a child's logic is: "I am being hurt . . . Bad children are punished . . . I must be bad . . . I am to blame for this." If the child is told that he is responsible for the abuse, then he is left in no doubt.

Many survivors of abuse carry a heavy burden of assumed guilt. Self-blame often represents an old belief system, and we have explored just how resilient these can be; so this conviction is not easily shifted. Self-blame gives rise to other feelings too, such as shame, which can fill a person with self-loathing and spoil relationships; guilt and the fear of being found out; a deep sense of being "bad"; and anger towards oneself which can be very destructive.

> *"I could have told someone about the abuse: I should have. I blame myself that the abuse continued for a year."*

> *"Mum told me that I had shamed the family by being born. I knew that it wasn't my fault that I was a child of incest but she hated me for it. She hated me so much that I assumed that I was bad and I felt shameful."*

> *"No one actually told me that I was to blame or that it was my fault, but no one protected me. Dad let his best friend molest me for money and my mother knew about it. When your own parents let something like that happen, you assume you deserve it and if you deserve it, you must have brought it on yourself."*

If you blame yourself for your abusive experiences, this chapter will help you to consider alternative possibilities.

Letting Go of Self-Blame

Letting go of self-blame may seem like a good thing, but it can be a difficult and painful step forward. Before you do start to challenge the idea that you are to blame for your abuse, think about the consequences of letting go of it. It is easy to appreciate the advantages of not blaming oneself – freedom from guilt and no longer being angry with oneself; no longer feeling different from others and morally "bad," and so on. However, letting go of self-blame can cause stresses which you need to consider. Below are a few examples of the dilemmas which can arise:

> *A man who no longer feels responsible for his abuse might have to accept that someone else was responsible. This might mean facing the shocking fact that an aunt chose to abuse him and his mother turned a blind eye to his suffering. Adjusting to something like this can be painful and frightening, stirring up feelings of betrayal.*

A woman who is in a bad relationship, but who no longer feels responsible for her abuse, might start to question that relationship. As she lets go of her feelings of worthlessness and badness, she might believe that she deserves better and that she is no longer prepared to work at a relationship which is abusive. She might eventually have to face the stress of ending the relationship and planning a new future.

A person who has accepted blame in the past, and who has suffered and harmed herself because of this, might discover new feelings of rage as she realizes that she was not to blame. She might unlock very strong feelings of anger when she reviews her suffering and she will have to learn how to deal with these emotions if she is going to protect herself from further hurt.

A middle-aged man has accepted blame since he can remember. His life had been limited, but he could accept this as part of his "punishment." When he began to see his experiences in a new light and began to shed his feelings of self-blame, he was gripped by a terrible grief that he'd wasted his life.

Exercise

- Imagine how you will feel about yourself, others around you and your future when you are able to let go of self-blame.
- Try to identify the stresses that this might create for you.

Adjustment to letting go of self-blame takes time, so pace yourself through this section and allow yourself enough time to get used to the implications. When you are going through times of re-evaluation, remember to use your coping strategies, developed in Chapter 10; nurture yourself and be ready to turn to your friends to help you deal with the stress. Before you do an exercise, it is probably a good idea to consider what you will do if you get distressed: have a plan and use your coping skills.

Understanding How Abuse Occurs

It was established some time ago, by an American researcher named David Finkelhor, that there is a particular pattern in abuse, whether this is physical, sexual and/or emotional.

- First, **the abuser** must want to abuse.
- Secondly, **the abuser** must overcome his/her inhibitions to abuse.
- Thirdly, **the abuser** must create an opportunity or an environment where abuse can occur.
- Fourthly, **the abuser** must *choose* to go through with the abuse: only the abuser can make this decision.

For example:

- The abuser might want to abuse in order to feel powerful, or because s/he wants to be intimate and has a distorted notion of closeness; or perhaps the abuser wants to cooperate with an abusive partner. There can be many reasons.
- Next, the abuser might overcome any inhibitions by believing that children's feelings are unimportant, or that children actually enjoy sex, or that youngsters will forget being beaten. Alternatively, the abuser might overcome inhibitions by getting drunk or drugged.
- The abuser might then create an opportunity for abuse by offering to baby-sit, or by taking a job involving contact with children, or befriending a lonely schoolchild, for example.
- Now the abuser is in a position to exploit a child; and only s/he can make the choice to go through with this.

At this point, *the child is at risk of abuse.*

The abuser must next overcome the inhibitions of the child – through blackmail, threat, bribery or clever persuasion. Certain experiences make any child much more vulnerable to being targeted for abuse: being lonely and isolated, feeling unloved, having a fear of adults, or having been abused before so that it just seems as if "this is what happens to me." You might want to consider what circumstances and experiences made you particularly vulnerable.

Exercise

- Why might you have been particularly vulnerable to being abused?
- Now, think about your abuser or one of your abusers and try to consider:

  Why did s/he want to abuse?
  How did s/he overcome her/his inhibition?
  How did s/he create an opportunity?

- Remember that the person who abused you then *chose* to go through with the abuse.

If, in doing this exercise, you find that your perspective has shifted, give yourself some time to adjust before moving on to the next section.

Assigning Responsibility

In order to take the blame for something, we have to assume responsibility for it. This section will help you to consider "responsibility" with regard to your abuse.

Two American psychologists, Dr Christine Padesky and Dr Dennis Greenberger, remind us that we can't draw conclusions about blame until we have considered *all* those who have some degree of responsibility for something happening. Therefore, make a list of all those who played a part in your abuse. Their part need only be minor for their name to be included in your list. Don't include your name yet.

For example:

- My teacher (who ignored my pleas for help)
- The church (which gave me my belief that I should always obey adults)
- My parents (for not disciplining my brother)
- My mother (for making it so difficult for me to confide in her)

- Social services (for not seeing what was happening in our family)
- Jim, my brother (who raped me)
- Jim's schoolfriend, Alan (who knew and never said anything)
- Jim's schoolfriend, Peter (who knew and never said anything)
- Jim's schoolfriend, Colin (who knew and never said anything)

Now, make your own list. Next, rank your entries, putting the person/organization that is most responsible at the top and the person or organization that is least responsible at the bottom. This will help you to shift the focus away from yourself for a while.

Order of responsibility

Most responsible	1 ....
	2 ....
	3 ....
	4 ....
	5 ....
	6 ....
	7 ....
	8 ....
	9 ....
Least responsible	10 ....

Now that you have considered all those involved, decide whether or not it is reasonable to add your own name to the list. Look at your entries and then consider how fair it is for you to carry as much blame as you do.

Empathizing With an Abused Child

The next step in examining self-blame involves reviewing things while holding in mind the vulnerability of a child. If it is difficult for you to realize just how vulnerable you were at the time of the abuse, see if you can find a photograph of yourself at the age when you were abused. Only do this is you feel able to manage the feelings that it might provoke. If you can't use a photograph of yourself, you could try looking at pictures of other children of that age in order to remind yourself of a child's vulnerability.

An exercise that can help you take this further involves writing a sympathetic letter to a hypothetical abused child who shared your experiences.

LETTER TO AN ABUSED CHILD

Dear Ricki,

I know that your parents tell you that you are a "big boy" and that your mum expects you to look after your little sister, but you are only a child and it's not fair that your parents put so much responsibility on your shoulders. I can understand that you must feel responsible and you feel that you have to be grown up, but you are too young to carry such a burden.

It's no wonder that you kept quiet about your abuse after the teacher told you that it was your fault in the first place, and that it was now your responsibility to keep quiet and "Act like a man!" But he was wrong to say these things to you. He bullied and blackmailed a child who simply wanted to do the right thing by everyone.

It wasn't your fault that you were abused: it was the teacher who chose to exploit you, and he was wrong to do that. It wasn't your fault that you said nothing: you had been manipulated by an adult and, anyway, your parents never wanted to hear about your problems. So who could you have turned to?

None of this should have happened to you. You are a nice kid, who does his best. You should have been protected from all the hurt that you suffered. If I could, I would protect you now.

Exercise

- Imagine a child who is the age that you were when you were abused. If this is difficult, look at a picture of another child of that age, as this can help you to get a feel of a child's size and vulnerability. Give this child a name and imagine that she or he has been abused in the way that you were.

- If you can, write a letter to that child, explaining why it is the abuser, and not the child, who is responsible. Let the child know that s/he is innocent. By doing this, you will help yourself develop an understanding of the child in a non-judgmental way.

- If you have been hurt by several people, or if your abuse spanned years, you might find that you write several letters to "children" of different ages. As a guide when you write, ask yourself , "What does a child need to hear in order to feel better?"

- If you can, imagine that child is you and, if it helps, address the letter to yourself. If it is too early for you to write to yourself, don't rush, just come back to the exercise when you feel ready.

By writing this letter, you not only continue to question blame, but you begin to soothe and comfort the hurt child. This is a crucial part of recovery. If you are distressed rather than comforted by the exercise, remember your coping skills. Also give yourself credit for being able to get in touch with the child in you.

Why I Was Not To Blame

By now, you might have developed some new ideas concerning blame. If you feel that you have begun to shift the old belief: "I was to blame," you could begin to reinforce this. Start by reviewing the assumption that you might be to blame for your abuse by looking at the evidence for and against this belief – just as you did in Chapter 13. First, write down the reasons why you feel that you *were* to blame, so that you can better understand why you hold this belief. Then, try to take an objective view and question these arguments and list the reasons why you *were not* to blame.

This is often a difficult exercise, so allow yourself time to come up with your challenging statements. At first, you might need help from others in order to undermine your thoughts of self-blame.

Below are some examples:

Why I thought I was to blame	*Why I was not to blame*
Because I let him touch me.	I was NOT to blame because I was frightened into doing things that I did not want to do.
Because I did not tell anyone.	I was NOT to blame because he threatened to harm me if I told.

Aim to come up with a challenging statement that really argues your case, again using the guidelines in Chapter 13 to help you. For example:

I **understand** that I felt to blame because I was always told that it was my fault and no one contradicted that.

However, I realize that I was not to blame, it was my abuser who was twisted and sick and he made himself feel better by blaming me.

Therefore, I'm not going to carry the responsibility for my abuse any longer, but I am going to have to learn to deal with the anger that this leaves me with.

Cycles of Abuse

Some survivors of childhood abuse suffer an additional burden of guilt because, at some time after their own experience of abuse, they have abused someone, or believe that they have. This might have been emotional, physical or sexual abuse of a partner or a child, for example. The abuse might be the result of misdirected anger, misunderstood displays of affection, or an aggressive response to feeling fear, for example. Memories of hurting someone, added to personal memories of abuse, may contribute to a very negative self-image and a profound sense of badness or worthlessness, so it is important to review this rather than trying to ignore it.

At different times in our lives, we have different perspectives and we behave differently. We may well look back and feel unhappy with the way we were. Being a good person does not mean that you will never do bad things: we all make mistakes and we all violate our own code of practice from time to time. You have to judge yourself fairly.

If you really have done something wrong, it is important not to deny it, but to understand why it happened and then to decide whether or not you can repair the damage. Realize that your actions do not confirm that you are bad or that you are an "abuser," and don't fear that if you understand, or even forgive, yourself you will have lost your standards or principles. By understanding yourself, you are not saying what you did was OK, you are recognizing that you did something that was not OK. Forgiving yourself requires a realistic appraisal of yourself: your good and your less good qualities. Be frank, because forgiveness should be more than a comforting, glib acceptance of our behaviors.

By recovering from the effects of your own abuse, you can heal the feelings of anger, confusion, hurt and betrayal which could have led you to misuse someone else. Then you can begin to forgive yourself, while recognizing that you have hurt someone.

Exercise

Again, if you feel that you have abused others, a writing exercise may be helpful. This exercise can be a very emotional one, so remember your coping strategies and use them if you need to. You could use the following format:

LETTER TO SOMEONE THAT I HAVE ABUSED

> *Dear...............,*
>
> *I am sorry for what I did to you. Please understand that . . .*

You may choose to send this letter, or you may choose not to.

Further Reading

There are few texts which focus on dealing with "blame," but you might find it helpful to read the biographies of other abuse survivors, as this could help you review your ideas about blame and responsibility.

There are very many such autobiographies on the market, but the following have been particularly popular:

I Know Why The Caged Bird Sings, by Maya Angelou (Bantam, 1983; Virago, 1984)

My Father's House, by Sylvia Fraser (Virago, 1989)

Cry Hard and Swim, by Jacqueline Spring (Virago, 1987)

15

Anger: Feeling It and Dealing With It

What Is Anger About?

Anger, like anxiety, can be a good thing if it is expressed appropriately. It is usually triggered by our being disrespected or frustrated, and it helps us assert and protect ourselves. Like anxiety, it is fuelled by adrenaline and makes us feel more "on edge" and more easily aroused as the body prepares for "fight or flight." Sometimes, indeed, anger is mistaken for anxiety.

Some of you probably survived your abuse because you did not let yourselves feel anger; in fact, many survivors don't let themselves feel at all. However, you might begin to get in touch with your own anger as you come to realize the effects of what happened to you; that it was unjust and that you were not to blame. On the other hand, it might be some time before you experience anger. Don't worry if you are not in touch with it; you can't force emotional reactions, but you can prepare yourself for them.

Like anxiety, anger can work against us if it is bottled up, exaggerated, misdirected or ignored, or if it is triggered by essentially harmless remarks or situations. Spend a moment imagining what happens if we ignore or bottle up our anger, or if we express it too readily.

Typically, bottling up or ignoring anger does not remedy the situation: we still have to tolerate the sensations of anger, and these tend not to diminish. Instead, they tend to build up and we have to deal with the increasing stress within us. This stress sometimes spills out, so that either our anger is not expressed respectfully or it is directed towards the wrong person: we are all familiar with the phenomenon of "kicking the cat" – directing anger at someone or something that doesn't deserve it – which isn't fair and which puts relationships at risk. Similarly, if we express anger too readily, if we have a "short fuse," we risk offending and alienating people unnecessarily, particularly those close to us.

So, it is important to learn how to *manage* anger and to use it only to advantage. Anger management is not about suppressing anger: it's about learning to recognize anger and then showing it in a reasonable way.

First, we need to be able to recognize anger. It is not unusual for anger to be confused with other emotions that we associate with adrenaline: fear and excitement, in particular. We have already said that the sensations of anger and anxiety are similar, and it is especially easy to confuse anger and fear if you have a fear of anger. Many children do learn that it is "wrong" to show anger and they grow afraid of it, fearing that if they show anger they will be punished or rejected. They never have an opportunity to learn that anger is a natural emotion and that there are acceptable ways of expressing it.

> *I begin to feel sick in my stomach and I'm thinking, "No. I can't handle this." Then I back down quickly. It's only later that I realize that I should have been angry, and then I turn it all on myself.*

Sometimes anger is mistaken for hunger. Both are associated with adrenaline and, for some, hunger feels like a safer, more manageable feeling.

> *If anyone had asked me, I would have said that I was a really placid, easy-going person. It was only in therapy that I realized that I did get angry with people but I avoided confrontation and I "ate at them" in secret. No wonder I battled with my weight.*

Some experience a thrill with anger: anger and excitement get mixed up, and expressing anger becomes exhilarating. Others feel a sense of power, sometimes for the first time in their lives. This is often the case for those who have difficulty controlling their anger. People with anger control problems are not usually angry all of the time and, between bouts of anger, they are typically perfectly amicable. However, when the adrenaline starts to flow, anger is mingled with feelings of excitement or power, and then it is very difficult to take stock of the situation and, perhaps back down.

> *I don't even know that I'm angry, but I know I start to get mean and I feel invulnerable for a while. I get sort of high and I feel nothing else.*

> *You don't have a childhood like mine without learning to look after yourself: I'm on the lookout all of the time. I'm a coiled spring and no one messes with me. That feels good.*

Understanding Anger

Sometimes feelings of anger can seem to be triggered by a particular person or situation. When this happens, we all need to ask ourselves: Is this really the person who has wronged me? Is my anger justified?

If you are unsure, or if your answer is "No," you need to explore just who or what has really triggered your anger and what the anger might mean to you. Only then can you begin to address the source of the feelings.

There are different types of anger to look out for: "primary", "secondary" and "past" anger.

Primary Anger   This refers to anger that is perfectly reasonable in the light of a current or past event. This anger focuses on a particular instance and is not influenced by past grudges and unresolved conflicts.

> "He stood there calling me a freak. He was totally out of order. I was angry with him for insulting me."

> "That young woman endangered my child, she worked at the nursery but she knew that she wasn't properly qualified. I was furious with her."

> "I'd worked really hard on that project and my boss cancelled it without consulting me. Of course I was mad."

Secondary Anger   This refers to anger that arises as a defence against hurt or fear. Dr Beck studied anger in the 1980s, and discovered that some anger is not primary, it is secondary to feelings of hurt or of fear. Anger becomes our protection against those feelings, and against further hurt or trauma. For example, a person might reason: *"While I'm angry, I can feel no fear,"* or *"My anger is my armour because others keep their distance,"* or *"If I'm not hostile, others will take advantage and abuse me again."* This kind of anger tends to arise very quickly, and it requires some effort to stand back and "observe" just what's going on.

> *"He only said that he disagreed with me on the one point, but it felt as though he was rejecting me. Before I knew it, I had walked off in a fury telling him to forget the whole thing."*

> *"When she said that, I could feel myself getting upset and I don't do that. I don't cry. I felt myself getting angry with her for doing this to me."*

> *"In broad daylight, he told me to move out of the way. I was worried that he was trying to intimidate me. I can't allow that to happen because if you show any weakness, you're lost. I felt a whoosh of adrenaline and I hit him."*

Past Anger   This is anger that we feel now, but which is really rooted in the past. Past anger can easily be triggered by today's frustration or offence, but the feelings we get are out of proportion to the immediate trigger.

> *"I saw the woman slapping her child in the street. I remembered all the times that I had been that child and I really lost my temper."*

> *"I had just begun to trust him when he casually mentioned an old girlfriend. Another man who is going to compare me with other women and play games. No thank you! I'd been there often enough, so I ended the relationship there and then."*

Directing Your Anger

It is important to recognize and express your feelings of anger rather than denying them, and it is important to direct the feelings towards those who have let you down rather than turning the anger inwards or directing it at the wrong person(s). It is all too easy to displace angry feelings for one person on to another person – "kicking the cat." This is usually very detrimental to good relationships and the social price of misplaced anger can be very high.

Monitoring Your Anger

Although it can feel good vent anger or to avoid it, you can damage your relationships and your self-esteem if you don't learn to express it in a way that is reasonable and respectful. So, you need to be able to analyze your reactions to ensure that you deal with anger appropriately

In Table 15.1 are some examples of the proper expression of anger being blocked by other feelings.

Table 15.1:   **Examples Of Anger Being Blocked**

Situation	Feeling	What was going through my mind
See a child being bullied	Anger turning to *panic*	This is stirring up all sorts of painful memories that I can't cope with
My husband took another woman out to dinner	Anger turning to *misery*	Anger is wrong. If I feel angry, this just confirms that I'm a lousy person. I shouldn't get mad at him anyway – its my fault that he needs to see other women, I'm so unattractive
John said something racist at the meeting	Anger turning to *embarrassment*	I shouldn't have shown that I was angry in public, I probably made others feel uncomfortable. They probably think badly of me now
Discovered that my school had known about the abuse and had turned a blind eye to it	Anger turning to *terror*	I mustn't feel like this, I can't control it. I'll go off my head and get violent if I don't stop it. Then I'll lose the kids for sure. I might even get put away
A youth threatened me on the street	Anger turning to *confidence*	I'm not feeling scared now. I feel powerful, like I can't be hurt. I'll show him

---

Exercise

- When you experience anger, you need to try to take stock and ask yourself what it's about. The mood and thought records that were introduced in Chapter 13 will help you to do this.
- If you can't "unpack" your feelings at the time, try to review them as soon as you can.
- The more you understand about your anger, the more in control you will be.

You can take this analysis forward in several ways, choosing whichever is most useful to you at the time. You can continue to keep records of "What I did" and "How helpful was this?" so that you can make a better analysis of the way you handle anger and if this is helpful. For example, the first two instances in Table 15.1 might be recorded as follows:

What I did

I panicked and, because I felt that I couldn't cope with the memories, I went back to my car and drove home

I felt so miserable and unattractive that I didn't say anything to my husband and I just acted as though it was OK with me

How helpful was this?

Initially, I felt relief, but the memories are still with me and now I'm even more afraid of going out. So I don't think it was helpful

I felt worse and worse over the next few days and I got really depressed. Pretending that I wasn't angry made me miserable

Or you might choose to ask different questions, like "What was going through my mind?" and "How would I view the situation, now?". The statements in Table 15.1 illustrate the thinking biases which you came across in Chapter 13, and you will find it helpful to identify these in your own automatic thoughts. Then you can go on to exploring your thoughts using the six questions that you also learnt in Chapter 13.

What was going through my mind?	What were my thinking biases?	How would I view the situation now?
I shouldn't have shown that I was angry in public, I probably made others feel uncomfortable. They probably think badly of me now	Jumping to conclusions: mind reading	What John said was unacceptable and one of us needed to make that clear. I was reasonable to feel and show anger and I probably expressed what others were thinking. It should be John who feels embarrassed
I mustn't feel like this, I can't control it. I'll go off my head and get violent if I don't stop it. Then I'll lose the kids for sure. I might even get put away	Catastrophizing	It's normal to feel angry in these circumstances. I can calm myself and deal with these feelings: although I do need more practice
I'm not feeling scared now. I feel powerful, like I can't be hurt. I'll show him	Emotional reasoning: I *feel* powerful	It's reasonable to feel angry, but this sense of power is not real and stops me from dealing with the situation in a reasonable way. One of us could get hurt, so I must walk away until I'm calmer

---

Exercise

Look out for misjudgments in your own records and go on to challenge inaccurate statements, substituting something more balanced responses.

By keeping a record of your levels of anger, you can also look for patterns that help you understand your anger better. You may identify certain times, persons and situations that render you more vulnerable to feeling angry. For example, a woman might have angry outbursts after she has bottled up her dissatisfaction rather than expressing it, or pre-menstrually, or when a person has let her down, or when she is in a threatening situation, and so on.

Understanding these links can help you better plan how to manage your anger. The woman in the above example might try to express dissatisfaction rather than bottling it up; she might take things more easy when she knows that she will be pre-menstrual; she might learn to assert herself with those who let her down and she can learn ways of managing her fears in certain situations.

Feeling Anger

Feeling anger towards someone who has abused or neglected you is natural, but it's often more complicated than that. You might have mixed feelings towards an abuser because you shared both good and bad experiences with them, or because you feel that you can "explain" or understand the abuse or the neglect; you might find yourself saying: ". . . but she only did it because she was so stressed herself" or ". . . he didn't really know what he was doing, he was always so drunk" or " . . . it was his way of showing that he cared."Understanding an action doesn't mean that you have to accept it or that it was excusable. You can still feel angry.

> "I realize that Dad was very stressed, raising three kids on his own, and I admire him for trying, **but** I'm still angry that he drank so much and that he beat us for the slightest thing."

You might feel numb rather than angry, or you might be so uncomfortable with anger that you have developed ways of "switching it off." Remember not to force feelings of anger; but if you do feel that it is the right time for you to try to get in touch with it, the following exercise may help.

Exercise

- Imagine yourself as a child. Try to get a vivid picture of yourself, noting how young you were; use a photograph if this helps.
- Then, think about what was done to you. Think about what you were forced to do.
- Consider the losses in your life and the missed opportunities, the unhappy years and the struggle to heal today.
- What do you feel?

If you get in touch with feelings of anger only to discover that you are scared by them, use your grounding skills (developed in Chapter 11) to help you take control of the situation. When you grow confident that you can feel angry but that you can ground yourself, you will find it less frightening to stay with the anger for longer periods of time.

If you are feeling very angry and showing it, you might want to discuss this with those close to you so that they will understand your feelings, and perhaps, your behaviors. You should also be thinking ahead and preparing to manage your anger so that you do not undermine the relationships you have formed.

Sometimes, venting anger simply feels good. After all those years of suppressing it, it can seem to be liberating to let go. Beware of this damaging your relationships and your self-esteem.

Dealing With Anger

If you have begun to monitor your reactions when you are angered, you might be able to answer these questions:

- What do you usually do with your feelings of anger?
- Do you express them as anger or do you experience them in other ways, such as fear, hunger, the need for a drink, the need to withdraw?

- Where is your anger directed – towards the abuser, towards yourself or towards someone who does not deserve your anger?

It is rarely easy to answer these questions at the time: you most likely just have a strong urge to get out of a place, or a powerful desire for a drink, for example. However, we can sometimes answer these questions when we reflect on events some time later. Look at the times you feel fear, or overeat, or have urges to harm yourself. Do any of these link with anger?

When you can say: "I am angry", you have to be able to do something with the feelings. In Chapter 17 ("Communicating With Your Family"), we will look at assertiveness skills, which will help you show your angry feelings in a controlled and re-spectful way. In addition, there are techniques that can help you *express* the raw feelings of anger which can obstruct being assertive. These are cathartic, physical activities which would include:

- pounding pillows with your fists
- playing vigorous sports
- tearing up newspapers
- screaming in a private place

These strategies will help you get the raw feelings out of your system, rather than bottling them up. However, you should always find something soothing to do immediately afterwards, so that you properly calm yourself. You could listen to music, take a warm bath, try a meditation or relaxation exercise. Then, you can decide whether you want to take your anger further. It is always easier to make a good decision about expressing anger when you have worked through the initial, raw feelings. That is why parents are advised not to discipline their children when they feel very angry, but to let the peak of the anger pass and then decide what it's best to do.

If you do decide that you want to express your anger towards a particular person, that this is the appropriate person and that this is safe for you to do, there are both indirect and direct methods of doing so, for example:

- writing down your feelings and thoughts
- writing a letter to the person who has angered you
- making an assertive telephone call
- having a (well-planned) face-to-face meeting

Indirect Expression of Anger

"Indirect" means not having to encounter someone face-to-face. This might involve having a "conversation" in your mind with the person who has wronged you; role-playing a confrontation with a friend; or writing a letter.

The indirect approach is not a cowardly route; it might be the right way for you at a certain time. It is certainly the right approach if your safety would be endangered by your facing the person with whom you feel angry.

Writing a letter can be particularly useful. Think of the person with whom you feel angry – this might be the abuser or the person who did not protect you – and then write down what you believe s/he should hear.

Below is an example of such a letter.

> *Dear Mother and Father,*
>
> *I am writing to you as a thirty-year-old man who has been through many years of unhappiness, failed relationships and a drink problem. It is only in the last year that I have realized that much of this has to do with you.*
>
> *I am angry with you because you did not shield me from the abuse which my grandfather put me through; you did not protect me from the sexual molestations of my uncle; you did not stop any of my hurt even though you must have known it was going on. Even now, you deny the significance of my childhood torment and tell me to try to forgive and forget. Nothing has changed and I'm angry with you for that, too.*
>
> *I don't know why you felt that something was more important than caring for your child. There is probably an explanation but I won't accept that as an excuse. I am moving*

*on now and, if you can't support me, I am going to have to
leave you behind.*

If you write a letter, you don't have to send it. You can hide it,
burn it, shred it or whatever makes you feel most comfortable.
The important thing is that you have expressed anger towards a
person who merits it.

Direct Expression of Anger

There will be times when you choose to express your anger
directly to the person who has triggered it. This might well require
planning and preparation, and you will find the next chapter on speaking out and confrontation helpful. So, if you are considering confrontation, read Chapter 16 first: this will help you to plan more
thoroughly. It is important that you always think of your safety:
don't risk directly confronting someone who might hurt you.

If you do confront someone with your anger and the situation does not go according to your plan, do two things:

• Have a contingency plan ready. Be sure to have thought about
the things that could go wrong and how you would handle
this.
• Try to focus on your achievements, learn from the experience and give yourself credit for taking on a difficult task.

Once you have expressed your anger and directed it away
from yourself, or others who don't deserve it, try to engage in a
soothing activity to help you achieve a feeling of calm. Self-
soothing is an important part of anger management.

Exercise

• Don't just assume that you will be able to think of ways
of dealing with your anger when you're angry: this is
often the time you're least likely to be able to come up
with anything.

continued on next page

- Instead, think now of the ways that would work for you and list them where you can find them when you need to.

Further Reading

The following books can give you some more ideas about dealing with anger effectively:

The Dance of Anger by Harriet Goldhor-Lerner (HarperCollins, 1997; Thorsons, 1990)

Managing Anger, by Gael Lindenfield (Thorsons, 1993; audio cassette – Harper Audio, 1998)

Anger: The Misunderstood Emotion by Carol Tavris (Touchstone Books, 1989)

16

Choosing to Speak Out or to Confront Someone

Many abused children are afraid to tell anyone what has happened to them, while others reveal their abuse only to find that their painful experiences are minimized or, worse, disbelieved. It makes sense that a child who is afraid or who feels unsupported cannot speak out. Some survivors carry such fears into adulthood, when it still feels too dangerous to speak out, let alone confront the person(s) who abused or neglected them.

Speaking Out

It is your choice whether you decide to speak out or not. Don't let anyone force you to do this; you have to make your own decision, in your own time. Ultimately, you might decide not to speak out, but to get on with your recovery privately. To help you make your decision, in this section you can look at the process of speaking out and what it means to you. Start by reflecting on the obstacles that have stood in the way of you telling others about your abuse (past and present). There will be reasons for not telling others, for example:

If I tell the police, I'll have to get involved in legal proceedings that I can't face
If I tell my family what happened, they'll hate me
If I tell my girlfriend, she won't believe me
If I tell my husband, he'll be disgusted by me
If I start talking about my abuse it will stir up too much in me

If I start talking about my abuse, I'll upset too many people
*My GP would never believe me because she's friendly with my
    family*
If my dad knew, he'd kill my uncle
I feel too ashamed
*This could get out of hand and I'd end up having to testify in
    court*

There are also good reasons for speaking out. Try to think what
you might gain from sharing more of your experiences. For
example:

If I tell my family I give them the opportunity to support me
If I tell my girlfriend, she might understand me better
If I tell my husband, he might help me get through this
If I tell someone, I won't feel so alone
If I say something now, I could protect others
I am tired of holding the family's secret, I need a break
*By not telling, I'm protecting my abuser and that makes me
    feel worse*

Speaking about your abusive experiences shouldn't be an "all-
or-nothing" venture. Don't go into it thinking that you have to
tell everything to everyone. It's your choice whom you tell and
how much you share.

Even if you decide not to share your history at present, think
hard about the person(s) that you might confide in: you need
to feel that they are trustworthy. You might find your confidant within your family or within your social circle, or you
may choose to confide in a professional such as your doctor,
someone from the police or a teacher whom you learnt to trust
in the past. Try to order the names that you come up with,
according to how much you would trust them. The reason for
doing this is as a reminder that there are those in whom you
could confide, if you chose. It's also a reminder that even our
friends are not equally trustworthy and you should try to
appraise how much you can trust a person before you consider sharing your history.

The process of deciding whether to tell or not should not be
rushed and may take a long time. When you have decided that

you are ready to tell, and you have considered whom you might tell, you need to think how you would go about it.

Preparing To Tell Someone What Happened

There are many ways of telling someone what happened. You may choose an indirect method, such as a letter or a telephone call, or you may feel that face-to-face disclosure is best. You will probably find it easier to tell one person at a time.

Speaking out invariably involves others and their reactions can vary widely. The person in whom you confide could be understanding, but could also be rejecting, cool, outraged, shocked or repelled. If this is a close friend, or a family member, the shift from supportive to aggressive or cold can be particularly painful.

Whenever you take on a challenging task, it's best to plan. This might seem like an obvious piece of advice, but many of us don't prepare ourselves well enough and face difficulties as a result. As a first step in breaking the silence, write down a plan of how you intend to go about it. Be as specific as you can, considering:

- Who will this involve?
- When is the best time for you?
- Where is the best place?
- What will you say?
- What could go wrong?
- What's your plan for dealing with this?

The consideration: "What will you say?" is very important. The last thing you want to happen is that you "dry up" and have nothing to say after all the effort and stress that will have gone into planning to speak out. You might have a general idea about what you want to say, but if you get nervous, you might get mixed up or simply forget what it was. Most people who know that they have to speak under pressure will prepare a script. The best man at his brother's wedding and even the seasoned Oscar winner will have thought through their speeches very carefully and will have practised until the words are extremely familiar. It will be helpful if you can do this too. The idea isn't that you will perform like an actor, but that you will be familiar and comfortable with what you want to say – so that, even if you get nervous and stressed, you will still be able to relay the essence of what you intended to say.

It can also help to rehearse what you intend to do, in your imagination. Again, this will familiarize you with your task and make it less frightening.

Don't avoid thinking about what could go wrong: thinking about the worst-case scenario is always a good idea if you are going to engage in something unpredictable. Use this to build a back-up plan (or more than one, if necessary). If your disclosure goes well and you don't have to resort to your back-up plan, then it's a bonus – but do be prepared.

Confronting

Confronting those who hurt or neglected you means being assertive and honest with them. In doing so, you acknowledge and respect your own position and your own needs. Being confrontational means being frank about your abuse, your feelings and the way that this has affected your life, but it doesn't mean that you will be aggressive or disrespectful. You don't have to be hostile in order to confront someone.

Once again, the decision to confront or not is yours. Some books or therapists might tell you that you have to confront your abuser(s) in order to recover. This is not the case: many of our clients have recovered from abuse without addressing those responsible. So, it is something that you can choose to do *if it is in your best interest*. It should be done because it is of benefit to you, and not because you intend to hurt or manipulate others.

As with "speaking out," you need to look at the pros and cons of confrontation. The pros, for example, might include:

I want to protect my children from abuse
I have the right to tell this man how much he has damaged my life
I want her to know that I have remembered what she's done: I'm not going to pretend any more

The cons, on the other hand, might include:

I think that he is still violent and it would be dangerous to provoke him

I don't know what the consequences will be and that's frightening

I risk my family banding together and rejecting me: I'm not ready for that yet

In thinking of pros and cons, you must consider whether the hopes that you have are realistic. Many survivors enter into a confrontation hoping that it will set things right: a negligent parent will become protective; a sister will divorce a brother-in-law; a cousin will apologize; you will be believed. These things might not happen, so you will have to examine your hopes and let go of those that are unrealistic.

Realistic hopes would include:

I will be able to tell my side of the story

I will be able to name my abuser within my family

Unpredictable hopes might include:

I will be believed

My father will take some action against my abuser

Unrealistic hopes would include:

We will all be able to put it behind us as if the abuse never happened.

Exercise

- Try to write down your hopes and then review them with a critical eye, asking yourself whether or not they are realistic.
- You might decide that some are realistic, while some are out of your control and thus unpredictable, and some are actually unrealistic.
- Look at your unrealistic and unpredictable expectations. Are there other ways of realizing these hopes? Will you have to let go of some expectations?

continued on next page

- If most of your expectations fall in the unrealistic and unpredictable categories, rethink confrontation: it might not be the right time for you to put yourself through it.
- You can always return to planning confrontation at a later date. There is nothing to be gained by taking on challenges prematurely.

Preparing for Confrontation

Confrontation can be anxiety-provoking and, at worst, it can be disappointing. None of us can force a person to change their opinion or behavior, and the person you confront could refuse to acknowledge your position. Remember that the point of confrontation, if you decide to go through with it, is that you will benefit, you will feel that you have moved forward.

Confrontation does not have to be in the form of a face-to-face meeting; indeed, if the person you want to confront is dead, inaccessible or dangerous, you will have to find other ways of doing it.

Indirect approaches which you might find helpful include:

- writing a letter (sent or unsent)
- making an audio-tape of the confronting statement, so you hear yourself saying what you want to say (again, you have the choice of sending this to the person who has hurt you)
- carrying out the confrontation in your imagination
- using the telephone, rather than face-to-face contact
- using a third party to convey the message

Confrontation can be dangerous. You do need to consider whether it is possible that the person you confront could become cruel and/or violent. If you do decide to confront someone who has hurt you, go through the steps for "speaking out," paying special attention to the preparation for things going wrong. The person who abused you was capable of hurting you in the past and might still be dangerous, so plan for safety if you are going to face your abuser.

Exercise

In preparing for confrontation, ask yourself:

- Whom do I want to confront?
- Why?
- What do I plan to say?
- Where and when (and with whom) is best for me?
- What's the worst thing that could happen?
- How do I plan to cope with this?

When you have done this groundwork, check out your plan with others, prepare yourself and go through it in imagination so that you can get used to how it will feel. If possible, use the support of someone trustworthy.

If the confrontation does not go according to plan, give yourself credit for trying, reflect on your achievement and learn from the experience.

About Forgiveness

As you work through your abusive experiences and begin to reach a feeling of resolution, you might begin to wonder whether or not you can forgive your abuser(s). Opinions on forgiveness vary: some feel that forgiveness is a necessary part of recovery, others believe that some things are simply unforgivable; some feel that forgiving an abuser helps them to achieve peace, others feel that forgiving lets the abuser off the hook and creates more stress.

You need to think about the meaning that forgiveness holds for you. If you decide that you do forgive your abuser, make sure that this is because you have recognized the abuser's strengths as well as weaknesses, that you have understood their frailties and limitations, that you have empathized with the abuser and have decided that you can forgive without demeaning your own position. Make sure that, in forgiving, you are not reinforcing your own sense of responsibility or self-blame, that you are not simply trying to resolve issues prematurely by "sweeping things under the carpet" through forgiveness, and that you are not "forgiving" because of social or religious pressure alone.

Forgiveness is not "all or nothing" – it doesn't have to be absolute. You can forgive some things in a person, but not others. You might find, for example, that you can forgive a teacher for not reporting your abuse to someone in authority, but not forgive him for behaving as if you had never told him about it; you might forgive a parent for neglecting her parental duties, but not for the physical and emotional hurt she inflicted on you.

Exercise

- If you have begun to think about forgiveness, set aside some time so that you can do this properly.
- Talk with others, write down your thoughts and make sure that you are making a real and personal choice in deciding to forgive or not.

As far as forgiveness is concerned, a most important step is forgiving *yourself* for having been abused. It is not *necessary* to forgive your abuser(s) or the person(s) who did not protect you. You might, or might not, reach an attitude of forgiveness, but you can still make peace with your past and move on.

17

Communicating With Your Family

Some of you might have been fortunate enough to grow up in a supportive family and you might have good relationships with family members. Others of you will have suffered abuse within your family and, as an adult, might still have difficulties in dealing with the family. Some family members can remain abusive and disrespectful, and if you want to remain in communication with your family, it's worth spending time learning how you can best deal with these difficult relationships. Many survivors would like to maintain some link with their family of origin, but without the disadvantages of feeling afraid or demeaned or exploited.

Sadly, after thorough review, some of you may find that the only way of dealing with the family is to cut off from it – at least in the short term. This can represent a huge loss, not only of actual contact with key people, but of hope. So many hope for the family that they never had, and it is hard if you have to accept that you never will have a family that is safe or respectful. So, in working through this section, you need to bear in mind that you could be moving towards reconciliation and better relationships, or you could be heading for significant compromise, or you could find yourself preparing to pull away from your family.

The Legacy of our Families

In Chapter 4, we looked at the way our belief systems and "mental filters" developed. It goes without saying that the environment in which we grew up, whether that was a family or an institution, influenced this enormously. Those of us who grew up in families learnt from this environment and, as adults, will be carrying around many belief systems which reflect those of our families. Some of these will be perfectly harmless, some will be helpful and some might be quite destructive. It is the latter that can handicap your progress and your lifestyle.

The sort of belief systems that can be destructive are those that prevent you from respecting, protecting or valuing yourself or others. In Chapter 13, we discussed the usefulness of trying to "catch" unhelpful beliefs and the automatic thoughts that are linked with them, so that you could review and, where appropriate, challenge them. This applies to family situations just as much as it applies in other settings; however, you might find that, within the family, it can be harder to put your finger on the thought or the belief that has just triggered feelings of distress or fear or hurt.

The reason for this is that the belief systems that we developed within the family go back a long way: so far back that they seem not to be represented as words that we can record; they are often more of a "felt sense" or a "knowing." What's more, these belief systems can be triggered by very subtle cues.

Joyce was the oldest child in her family, who had always been held responsible for the care of her sisters. She had done her best, but despite this, her mother always managed to let her know that what she did was not good enough.

As an adult, Joyce had become a successful businesswoman and was thought of as a capable, assertive and strong-willed manager. Each month, she drove 200 miles to visit her parents and she would describe feeling strong and competent until she walked into the family home.

"She doesn't say anything – it's just that disapproving look. I crumble inside and want to give up and hide. I feel like I'm eight years old again and that I'm stupid and I'll never get it right. It's as if she presses a button which taps into my worst feelings about myself."

> *Joyce is immediately transformed from a confident business-woman to a nervous child without a word being spoken.*

It is because our families so influenced our "inner world," and because our learning experiences within the family go back to infancy, that the family can have a powerful, immediate effect on us, sometimes without words being necessary. This can be a very good thing if the messages that a child receives are positive. Then, returning to the family home can feel healing and supportive, again without a word having to be spoken.

For example, if a family gives a child the messages: "You matter, we love you and we will do our very best to protect you," just being with that family can give instantaneous feelings of worth and safety, and walking through the front door of the family home can restore flagging spirits. If, on the other hand, a family gives the messages: "You disappoint us; we don't believe you; don't look to us for support," then contact with that family can trigger feelings of shame, anxiety and insecurity.

If you are going to tackle problem relationships within your family, you must first be able to recognize your vulnerabilities when you are with the family. For Joyce, it was a disapproving look; for someone else, it can be subtle criticism of their appearance; for another person the trigger is a conversation where their view is never acknowledged. As usual, self-monitoring can help you to get a handle on this.

My feelings	What triggered this
Useless, stupid	I'd hardly said a word before she rolled her eyes as if I was really stupid
Unimportant	Dad goes on and on, voicing his opinion and never asks what I think or how I am. If I try to say something, he dismisses it
Shame	The first thing she said was "You've put on weight"

Exercise

Begin to monitor your feelings when you are with family members.

Simply being aware of these processes can sometimes help you deal with the hurt. By being able to stand back, by detaching a little, you might be able to take the sting out of the experience. However, if this is not sufficient, you will need to think about ways of communicating your distress and asserting your needs so that you can maintain your integrity within your family. This can begin with your establishing some ground rules.

Establishing Ground Rules

In this section, you will have the opportunity to think about what you want or need from your family in the future. Sadly, it may be that they are unwilling or unable to meet your needs; but at the very least, *you* have respected your needs. As always, you will have the choice whether to maintain relationships or break them off.

The needs of a person within a family might include:

- I need to feel safe and loved
- I need to feel independent of my family
- I need to be comfortable in my own home
- I need to feel that my children are safe

Some of your ground rules will aim to meet your needs completely; others will represent a compromise. For example:

I won't take care of my father when he's drunk: then at least I'll be safe.

I'm not going to the family home in my vacations: I'm going to have a holiday.

*I'll meet him but I won't have my brother in my house, and
then I won't feel uncomfortable.*
*I'll let her visit, but I won't let my aunt be alone with my kids,
then they'll be safe from her.*

Exercise

- Start by listing your needs.
- Then look back over your list and think what you can do
  to make sure that your needs are met.
- These points will form your ground rules for dealing with
  your family.

It's likely that, as you write your ground rules, you will have
begun thinking: "Yes but . . . I couldn't leave my mother to deal
with my dad on her own . . . I could never explain to my father
that I didn't want to spend my holidays with him . . . I don't
know how I'll tell mum that I won't have her son in my house
. . . I can't deprive my kids the chance to see their cousins . . ."
The "Yes buts" are quite usual when any of us embarks on something new; they stop us from being too careless in what we do.
However, you need to catch them, review them and, if it's the
right thing to do, challenge them just as you would any other
unhelpful thought.

Another obstacle in asserting your needs is what Oprah
Winfrey recently called "the disease to please." She was refer-
ring to the drive to put others first, sometimes at great cost to
ourselves. If we constantly meet the needs of others, while
ignoring our own, we will burn out; we may become resentful
and we certainly won't get our needs met by others.

Common reasons for not asserting oneself are:

- People won't like me
- I'll be rejected
- I'll have to cope with the guilt trip
- I'll be compared (unfavorably) with my sister
- I shouldn't express my needs: I don't deserve it

Exercise

- Imagine a situation where you are asserting yourself, you are saying: "This is what I need."

- What uncomfortable feelings do you have?

- What are the thoughts that go with them?

- This will give you an idea of the obstacles that you will have to grapple with.

To make it easier for you to implement your ground rules, there are a few steps that you can follow which will help you be more assertive.

Asserting Yourself

You don't have to worry that asserting yourself means being hostile and insensitive – it doesn't. It's the aggressive person, not the assertive person, who thinks only of personal needs or desires without respecting the rights of others. You will have experienced this at the hands of your abuser(s). The assertive person is respectful of the rights of others, while keeping her/his own rights in mind. Assertiveness means communicating your needs in a way which is not aggressive, nor passive, nor manipulative. If you respect yourself, while respecting others, then you are being assertive. This is a crucial balance if you want to learn to get along with others. Without this balance you will be bullied or you will be the bully.

Although the first step in being assertive is a self-referential one: "What do I need or want?" the second is more circumspect: "Is this reasonable? Is this workable? Is this fair?" Then you can go on to generate a reasonable proposition which reflects a balance of your needs with the rights of others. Ultimately, what often follows is a compromise.

For example, Dana decided that she did not want to visit her parents' home again. She had been abused there, by a relative, and returning to the house upset her. Next, she considered the feasibility of not returning to the house. In never going back, she would disappoint her parents and risk not seeing her younger brothers, who lived there between school terms. So, she compromised and decided that she would only visit her parents' house when her younger brothers were there and that she would refuse all other invitations.

Just as with confrontation, being assertive does not have to involve a face-to-face interaction. You can be assertive in a letter, on the phone or through a third party. Dana did not want to confront her parents face-to-face nor speak to them on the telephone because she was sure that they would not hear her out, so she wrote a letter which explained:

> *Although you often invite me home and you might even think that I enjoy visiting you, I am writing to let you know that I find returning to the house where I was abused too upsetting. I have given this a lot of thought and I have decided that I shall be visiting less frequently in the future, and only when David and John are home. I hope that you will understand and respect my wishes, and that we can begin to work out ways of seeing each other that aren't too painful for me. If you trivialize how distressed I feel and are not prepared for me to visit when I choose, I can make arrangements to meet up with my brothers elsewhere.*

In this way Dana had been able to express her own needs, balance them with the preferences of her parents and the needs of her brothers, and then put forward a proposal for her parents to consider. She also added a sentence which explained what she felt that she would have to do if her parents did not respect her wishes. This is a helpful final step, reinforcing that Dana meant business. It wasn't a threat made to manipulate the family, but a statement which honestly set out an alternative way of handling the situation.

Exercise

In being assertive, you need to work through four steps:

1 Decide what you want or need
2 Decide what is reasonable and fair
3 Generate a reasonable proposal – which may represent a compromise
4 State the consequences of your proposal not being properly considered.

Being assertive is a sophisticated social skill and not one that is developed overnight. If you are going to be able to assert yourself, you really need to do the ground work by going through steps 1–4 described in the exercise. You might also find that you need to rehearse being assertive, with a friend or in front of a mirror, so that you can begin to feel more confident.

Once we have made our assertive statement, we hand over control to the other person(s), and we can't control how they react. Dana could not be certain that her parents would accept her proposal; she could only put forward a fair argument and have a contingency plan in place. If we are fortunate, our assertions are considered and we can work out something that is acceptable to everyone. If we are less lucky, we can be faced with opposition and manipulation, and we need to be ready for this.

Managing Opposition and Manipulation

Anyone who strives to be assertive is likely to come across opposition from time to time, so you need to be prepared for it. This happens within and outside families, but family members are often very good at undermining the efforts of the person who challenges the family's stability. This is not to say that you should expect opposition and manipulation, but that you should be prepared for it.

Some opposition is very direct and in the form of clear messages that you are not believed or not supported, while some opposition is more subtle and takes the form of emotional blackmail and re-directed blame. For example:

"This would kill your father – you'd better not tell him."
"How could you do this to our family? You've upset everyone."
"If you really cared about her/him/me you wouldn't be asking this."
"You brought these things on yourself: you've no right to make new rules now."

Or it could simply be "that look" from a disapproving relative.

In order to deal with these sorts of reactions, you will need to be able to stand your ground and, if you choose to, repeat your assertive statement. You need to be able to stay calm, so the stress management skills that you learnt in Chapter 10 are relevant here. Then, rehearse your statement until it's so easy to say that you will find it possible to repeat it calmly, again and again like a broken record.

Alternatively, you can accept that the other person is being manipulative and unfair and simply walk away with the knowledge that you have been reasonable. Remember, the goal in asserting your needs with your family (or anyone else, for that matter) is to address a situation without undermining yourself or others. The goal is not to "win": winning is a bonus.

Taking steps to change your relationships with family members involves a lot of courage. Do this at your own pace and make sure to ask for support from others that you trust.

Assertiveness Training and Further Reading

If you struggle with assertiveness, both within the family and outside family situations, consider joining an assertiveness training course; many local authorities and colleges run them. You can also do a lot more reading around this subject. The following are particularly good texts:

A *Woman In Your Own Right*, by Ann Dickson (Quartet Books, 1982; available through Amazon)

Assert Yourself, by Gael Lindenfield (Thorsons, 1997; audio cassette – Harper Audio)

When I Say No I Feel Guilty, by Manuel Smith (Bantam Books, 1975)

You might want to read more about families and their influence on us, in which case the following will be of interest:

Families and How to Survive Them, by R. Skynner and J. Cleese (Methuen, 1983; Oxford University Press, 1984)

18

Opening Up to Others

Anyone who has been hurt in the past, or who has poor self-esteem, might have problems in getting close to others or maintaining intimate relationships. If you have had little experience of feeling safe with others, especially "caring" figures, then you might well find it difficult to trust. If you had mixed messages, like: "If someone cares about me, they hurt me," or "If someone loves me, they show it sexually," then you might be very confused in close relationships, as well as being at risk of further hurt.

Neglected and abused children might never have been touched or held in a caring, safe way and they will not have learnt how to respond to someone who offers real tenderness. To them, tenderness might threaten pain.

It is natural to try to protect oneself from being hurt by others, and avoiding intimacy might seem like a way of achieving this. Unfortunately, this causes its own problems. It might feel safer, in the short term, to avoid close friendships, but most of us find loneliness painful and unrewarding.

For some time now, research has shown that those with good social support are less likely to suffer emotional problems, and those who have at least one confiding relationship are especially protected. So it is worth taking steps to increase your social circle and to foster close relationships, risky as this might seem.

By now, it won't come as a surprise to learn that the first step in achieving this is understanding more about your difficulties with intimacy.

Monitoring the Obstacles to Intimacy

Once again, you can use record keeping to help you identify the obstacles to you risking intimacy. Later, you can review your record and analyze your reactions, as you did in Chapter 13.

The aim here is to keep a record of your thoughts and reactions when you find yourself pulling away from a friend or ending a relationship. Sometimes you will realize that you are doing the right thing in withdrawing, but sometimes you might identify negative biases in your thinking and reactions based on fear or misconceptions. In this case you are probably not doing what is best for you, and so you need to give it some more thought.

Below are a few examples of misconceptions which can be challenged and rectified.

Automatic Thoughts	*Analysis*
1 Everyone has hurt me in the past, this person will, too. I'd rather get out now.	I'm overgeneralizing and I'm falling into my old pattern of running away as soon as I feel uncomfortable.
2 This person seems to like me, but that's because she does not know the real me. I can't stand the hurt of her realizing that I'm a lousy person so I'm going to pull out of this friendship.	I'm predicting the worst and mind reading. She is finding things about me that she likes, so I'm not all bad. I dislike some things about her and I still want her as a friend.
3 He let me down. That was an awful thing to do to me! I won't forgive him.	He's been a good friend for a year, this might have been a one-off. I can't assume that he doesn't have a good explanation.
4 I just don't feel anything for him. This must be a bad relationship.	I know that I have tended to disconnect from emotional reactions. This could be happening now.
5 I'm glad that I've been invited to the party, but I can't go because I just don't know how to behave and what to say in those situations. I'm pathetic and should stay at home.	I'm not pathetic, I'm just unskilled and unconfident because I don't have much social experience.

When you have reviewed your thoughts, you can work out what course of action would be in your best interest, for example:

Action

1 I'll take the risk and work on this relationship, knowing that I could always get out of it later. It still might not work out, but I will have given it a chance.

2 I'll try to focus on the things she might like about me. I might even ask her what they are. I'll remind myself just how good this friendship is for me.

3 I'll ask him for an explanation and give him another chance if he has a reasonable excuse. I will be wary, though.

4 I'll give the relationship more time, so that I can find out what I really feel.

5 I'll watch what others do and try to get some ideas. I'll try to find a book on social skills which could help me. I know that this will take time, and I should take things gradually.

Exercise

When you feel ready, start to monitor and analyze the obstacles that you come up against when you have the opportunity to get closer to someone.

Again, this exercise is putting you in control and preventing you from operating on the "automatic pilot" that might have jeopardized relationships in the past.

Building Up Your Social Skills

A consequence of never really getting close to others can be a lack of self-confidence in social situations. Lacking social skills and confidence presents a significant obstacle to developing any relationship, let alone a close one. By building your confidence in social situations, and learning to make conversation, you will be much more able to begin to get close to others.

Your assertiveness skills are already part of your social skills repertoire. If you are confident that you can respect your own needs and say "No" when you choose to, you will be more socially able. So revise the earlier section on being assertive within the family and translate the principles to your social and work life.

Observe those whom you know are socially skilled. You will probably see that they hold eye contact with others (but not too much), that they smile readily (but not too much), that they give compliments (but not too much) and that they use the other person's name (but not too much). You will be able to copy many of the social behaviors that you see in others and build up your repertoire this way. It can be particularly helpful to watch how others handle difficult situations and then adopt the successful approaches yourself. See how much you can learn from observing friends and strangers, or fictional characters in books, on the television or in the cinema. Make notes if you think that you'll forget what you have observed.

You can also ask others what they would do in certain situations. For example, if a colleague has suggested you join her for lunch, and you are not sure of her intentions or how to handle the situation, get someone else's perspective on this. Two heads are, generally, better than one.

When you are in social settings or you are spending time with one particular person, it is important that you feel comfortable with your social behaviors, so rehearse them whenever you can. Practice your smile in front of the mirror; try out friendly phrases with those with whom you feel comfortable, or get used to using these phrases with your colleagues rather than saving them up for special occasions. As always, it is a good idea not to take on the most difficult social challenge first, but instead to get used to using certain behaviors and phrases in "safe" environments until you feel confident enough to move onto more challenging situations.

Exercise

If you realize that you are socially anxious, then you can use the technique of catching your anxious thoughts, analyzing them and, where relevant, challenging them, just as you have done in other difficult situations. Use the same format as before, asking yourself:

1 "Just what are my anxious thoughts or images?" Be as precise as you can and use your diaries to help you.
2 "Are there biases in my view of things?" Look for distortions and exaggerations in your outlook.
3 "Is there evidence to support my thought or image?" Some of our upsetting thoughts are accurate, some are not and some have a grain of truth in them. What experience or knowledge do you have which fits with your distressing view of things?
4 "What is the evidence that does *not* support my thought?" Balance step 3 by reviewing your experiences and listing anything which you could use to argue against your original view. Think how someone else might view the situation. Ask yourself the following questions:

- Am I missing something important? Have I looked at all the facts?
- Have I had experiences that don't fit in with my upsetting thought?
- If someone else had this thought, what would I say to them?
- If I told my best friend about this thought, what would s/he say?
- When I'm feeling good in myself, how would I view the situation?

Further Reading

A book that is dedicated to helping you use cognitive behavioral techniques to deal with social anxieties is:

Overcoming Shyness and Social Anxiety, by Gillian Butler
(Robinson/New York University Press, 1999)

The Problem of Being Over-Intimate

So far, we have discussed problems related to intimacy as if they
always revolved around avoidance of intimacy, but problems can
also arise for those who become over-intimate too easily. Trusting too much can present as many difficulties as trusting too little; for example, we make ourselves very vulnerable to exploitation
and betrayal if we trust before we have good reason for doing so.

> *Some years ago, Sally hadn't any friends. She didn't want to
> take the risk of being hurt. In therapy, she had learnt that it
> might be safe to open up more and this felt liberating. She
> found herself opening up very quickly to her boss and to a
> male colleague, Joe. At first, Joe seemed supportive and she
> told him more of her history. As she confided more in him,
> he began to press her to begin a physical relationship. She
> realized that things were moving far too quickly and she
> tried to withdraw a little. Joe became angry and, to make
> things worse, he started to use his knowledge of her history
> to hurt her. He called her a "sad, weird, sexual misfit." It
> was as if he knew her worst insecurities and he was now
> using them against her. Too late, Sally realized that she had
> confided in this man without really knowing him. Fortu-
> nately, her boss was a different type of person who offered
> Sally genuine support when he saw her distress.*

If you find that you tend to rush into relationships and trust
others too readily, you can analyze this just as easily as you have
analyzed other patterns of behavior and automatic thoughts.

Automatic thought	*Analysis and action*
It feels so good to have a friend. I feel as though I've got so much that I want to tell her.	I understand that I am excited by the prospect of a friendship but I should hold back until I know her better. If the friendship is going to work, it will work even if I don't trust her completely.

He's been very open, so I really should tell him more about myself.	Being open was his choice and I won't put myself under pressure to match him. I want to take things more slowly.
This person is different, I can sense that he's decent and I can trust him.	My "senses" have let me down in the past. I could be right about this man but I should give him time to prove himself.

A final word about trust. This may seem obvious, but it is worth emphasizing that trust isn't an "all-or-nothing" thing. Although it is basic to healthy relationships, it can be given in degree and we can change our minds about the degree to which we trust a person.

If you consider a spectrum of trust running from 0% to 100%, think where you would put your acquaintances on the spectrum:

❑ .... ❑

Trust: 0%   50%   100%

Ideally, you should find names scattered along the spectrum, showing that you don't over-invest or under-invest in others. It is wise not to trust or to mistrust completely: unless you have *good evidence* for doing so.

If you don't have names in the middle region, ask yourself if your perspective is "all or nothing". If they are scattered at the 0% end, then you are probably avoiding intimacy. If they cluster around 100%, then you probably get over-intimate.

If you were to do this exercise in a year's time, you would expect to see some changes. As we learn more about those around us, we can adjust our views. For example, someone who seemed very trustworthy might let you down. You wouldn't necessarily put this person at 0%, but you might drop them down the scale. On the other hand, a person who hadn't shown particular loyalty in the past might stand by you and you might consider moving them up the scale a little.

In summary, trust is usually something that we give to a degree and which should be under constant review.

Communicating With a Loved One

In the 1980s, Dr Beck wrote a book about relationships called *Love Is Never Enough*. What he meant by this was that a good relationship is based on more than affection; it needs commitment and skill to survive. A primary skill in all relationships is communication.

If you have problems with trust, if you have a low self-opinion, if you have been hurt by someone that you love, you will find it difficult to open up to a loved one now. If you do not learn how to communicate with the person you are closest to, you can't share important things in the relationship. At worst, there could be confusions and misunderstandings that actually damage your relationship.

Even in the closest relationships, we can't expect to be able to "mind read" and we shouldn't expect it of a loved one. We really need to be able to say things and clarify situations so that misunderstanding don't develop. "Relate," the organization that used to be known as "Marriage Guidance," tells us that the ability to "tell" and to "listen" is crucial to a good relationship. This may seem obvious, but how often do you find yourself not saying what you really mean, or making something else the issue, or not talking at all, or changing the subject if a friend or partner tries to raise an issue?

Sometimes we fall back on these tactics because we have not really thought through what is bothering us, we just sense that it's uncomfortable and we'd rather avoid it. By now, this must be a familiar theme: the danger of acting on intuition rather than thinking things through. The way round this problem is the approach that we've continued to refer to in this book, namely:

- Monitor what is going on, however much you might want to avoid an issue
- Catch the automatic thoughts or images
- Analyze them
- Put into action what you have learnt about challenging misconceptions, managing anger and being assertive

This can help you have a more open and fair relationship, especially if your close friend or partner is also prepared to look more closely at her or his automatic reactions in the relationship. If the relationship is important to you both, there is good reason for you both monitoring the sticking points in your relationship.

Table 18.1 sets out a few example of the immediate reactions that can threaten a relationship, along with alternative ways of dealing with the situations.

Table 18.1	Communications in Relationships	
Feeling	*Thought*	*Alternative*
Jealousy, and this makes me frantic with worry	He's not phoned. He's broken his promise, probably because he's out with someone else	I could be over-reacting because I'm insecure. However, I don't know him that well and I could be right **Action: So I'll phone a friend for some moral support and advice. If he does ring, I'll tell him how upset I am, so that he will understand next time**
Leaden inside, really hurt	I've done so much to please her, and still she didn't really thank me. I don't want to think about it	This is tapping into the hurt I felt as a child when I was told that I wasn't good enough. I mustn't let this mess up my relationships now. **Action: I will ask Sheila if she appreciated my efforts, rather than trying to "mind read"**
Furious	She said that she'd be there for me and when I ask for help she tells me to "hang on" a while. That's the story of my life. Well I need help now, so she can push off	Perhaps she has a good reason for not coming over to help me right now. I know that I can be a bit pushy when I get into a panic, so I might have expected too much. **Action: I feel that I should visit and apologize for being rude and I can explain why I got so mad. I'll give her another chance**

Exercise

Use this familiar format when you experience a breach in your close relationships and take the opportunity to analyze just what is going on for you. Then think how best to take things forward.

The Natural History of Relationships

A last, but salient, point about relationships is that they are ever-changing. Rarely are we able to maintain the thrill of a new friendship or of an intimate relationship. The quality changes over time and that isn't a failing, it's natural progression. The initial attraction can turn to a more enduring affection, passion is gradually replaced by a deeper compassion, we can grow increasingly secure and emotionally intimate. These changes can bore the thrill seekers or frighten those who fear commitment and intimacy. If you want your relationship to last, you might find that you need to address any difficulties that you have adjusting to the change in its qualities. For example, when you feel "bored," ask yourself if you are really bored – perhaps you are so unused to security and familiarity that you struggle to adjust. If you feel fear in your relationship, try to analyze what it's about before you abandon your partner or close friend.

When we first establish relationships, we find the other person attractive in all sorts of ways. They have many qualities that we feel drawn to: their spontaneity, their honesty, their sense of the ridiculous, for example. When a relationship becomes strained, these exact same qualities can offend us: spontaneity seems more like carelessness, honesty seems brutal and unfeeling, a sense of the ridiculous seems childish. Once more, you might consider reflecting on this before you condemn your relationship.

Useful Contacts and Further Reading

Working on relationships, particularly those that are in difficulty, presents an enormous task and, if this task is too difficult to manage without extra support, consider contacting your local "Relate" counselling service. The telephone number will be in the directory. You will also find the following books helpful:

Love is Never Enough, by A. T. Beck (HarperCollins, 1989; Penguin, 1989)
The Dance of Intimacy, by H. Goldhor Lerner (HarperCollins, 1990; Thorsons, 1989)
The Relate Guide to Better Relationships, by S. Litvinoff (Vermilion, 1992)
You Just Don't Understand, by D. Tannen (Ballantine Books, 1990)

Your partner or a close friend might also find these books useful, as they have been written to help those close to survivors understand what is involved in recovery:

Allies in Healing, by L. Davis (Harper & Perennial, 1991)
Outgrowing the Pain Together, by E.Gil (Dell Books, 1992)

19

Managing Sexual Difficulties

Sexual difficulties are not uncommon: that is why you can find a large self-help literature on the subject and why there are professionals specifically trained as sex therapists. If you do experience sexual difficulties, you are certainly not alone.

Some survivors of abuse will find that they get into adult relationships which are abusive, emotionally, physically or sexually. To an outsider, this can look odd, and yet there are ways of understanding this. Others will avoid sexual relationships altogether and, again, there are ways of understanding this.

A proportion of survivors of abuse, particularly sexual abuse, avoid sexual contacts altogether because of fear and mistrust; others may have many sexual experiences yet take no pleasure in this; others have never learned to say "No" to sexual advances and experience sex only because someone else wants it. Some survivors cope with difficulties in sexual relationship by covering up their real feelings – for example, "spacing out" during sex or faking enjoyment. Some had their only close or affectionate childhood contacts through sex and now seek out sexual partners, almost indiscriminately. Others cannot bear to engage in sexual activity because it is too painful, physically or emotionally. Some men and women who have been sexually abused find that they are overwhelmed by memories when they have a physical relationship.

One of the reasons why so many struggle with sexual problems is the complexity of a sexual *relationship*. It's not just about sex. Our sexual relationships are influenced by the quality of our relationship with our sexual partner, and by the feelings that we have about ourselves and our bodies, and by our state of mind, and by our understanding of sex. Difficulties in any one of these areas can lead to problems in a sexual relationship.

Learning About Sex and Sexual Relationships

As we grow up, we generally begin to understand more and more about sex and about sexual relationships. The natural curiosity of children means that they ask questions, explore their own bodies and engage in mutual exploration with playmates. This natural accumulation of knowledge and understanding is often arrested in the abused child.

A "good" knowledge of the act of sex is not necessary for a good sexual relationship: many young couples start out sexually naïve and go on to have very fulfilling sexual relationships. However, misunderstandings about sex can be a major handicap to a physical relationship and having at least a basic and accurate understanding of sex can help.

Don't be critical of yourself if you feel unconfident about sex. Many people don't receive sex education at school and their parents never talk about "the facts of life." There is much to learn about sex that is very factual and books can help you gain a better knowledge quickly. There are now some excellent books on the market and I have recommended several at the end of this chapter.

Although sexually abused children are introduced to sex earlier than usual, as adults they can have a very poor knowledge of sex – the "physics" of it, how the average person reacts, what the average person wants, what can go wrong, how physical problems can be overcome, and so on. This is often because the child learnt to associate shame with sex and, therefore, doesn't ask the questions that the average child asks of parents and playmates.

OK, I realize now that Simon was a bad choice of partner, but there was a time when I trusted him. I told him about my cousin sexually molesting me when I was a kid and then Simon seemed to expect me to be really knowledgable and

> *adventurous when it came to sex. I felt like an absolute*
> *fool because I felt I knew nothing. I had just "tuned out"*
> *when she molested me and I felt so ashamed and dirty about*
> *sex that I couldn't even bring myself to read the school*
> *biology books.*

The sexually abused child can be particularly confused about
sex because some, but not all, experiences of sexual abuse are
tinged with pain *and* pleasure. Sometimes it's the pleasure of
having physical attention – the preliminary hugs, for example;
sometimes it's the pleasure of being made to feel special; sometimes it's sexual pleasure.

> *I was a handicapped child and people just aren't affection-*
> *ate towards the handicapped. So when my grandfather*
> *stroked me and asked me to stroke him, it felt good. I felt as*
> *though I was wanted. When he started to hurt me, I just*
> *sort of "floated out of my body" so I didn't feel the pain.*

> *There was no affection in my stepfather's abuse of me. He*
> *didn't speak, he just touched me and touched himself until*
> *it was all over. The whole experience was brutal and I would*
> *be hating it, when suddenly I would have these extraordi-*
> *nary feelings. I now know that this was an orgasm, but, as*
> *a child I just knew that if I waited long enough, there would*
> *be this amazing feeling. I hated him, but I began to look*
> *forward to the feeling.*

Our bodies are "programmed" to respond sexually. Just as we
are "programmed" to cough or sneeze when the lining of our
throat or nose is irritated, the human body should respond to
sexual stimulation. If you were masturbated or penetrated as a
child and you had an orgasm, you were not precocious, or dirty,
or strange, or to blame for your abuse; your body was respond-
ing in the way that our bodies are designed to respond.

All sorts of relationship problems can arise for adults who, as
children, experienced pleasure in an abusive relationship. For
example, they might seek out abusive relationships, trying to
recapture the pleasure which has become associated with hurt,
or they may feel tremendous guilt and, as adults, have difficulty

acknowledging pleasure with a partner because it is so tinged with shame.

Despite the struggles that survivors of abusive relationships might experience, they can change the quality of their sexual relationships and learn to feel comfortable about physical contact. You don't need to have a sexual partner to begin this work as you can learn much from reading and planning and beginning to enjoy your own body. However, if you have a sexual partner, the quality of your relationship with this person will influence your sexual recovery.

Relationships With Sexual Partners

As we saw in the previous chapter, relationships have to be worked at; this is particularly true of our sexual relationships. Trust, too, is even more important. Sexual trust is vital in establishing a good physical relationship with another person, so you need to consider what would help you to begin to trust that person. Just as you considered ground rules for improving your relationship with your family, think of the ground rules that you need in order to improve your sexual relationship. Start by reflecting on your needs, and then work out the ground rules which will help you meet them. For example:

My needs:

- I need to feel loved
- I need to feel equally in control
- I need to be comfortable in bed
- I need to feel that it's OK to stop having sex whenever I get uncomfortable
- I need to feel that it's OK not to have penetrative sex

As before, some of your ground rules will aim to meet your needs completely, others will represent a compromise.

Ground-rules:

- My partner and I will give each other compliments and we will say "I love you"

- My partner and I will agree that either of us can initiate sex and either of us can stop it
- It's OK for me to say "No", if I just want to sleep, or talk or cuddle
- We will discuss how I can say that I don't want to carry on during love-making, without hurting my partner's feelings
- My partner and I will talk about, and try out, other, non-penetrative ways of love-making

Your ground rules need to be shared and discussed with your partner, which can be a new and uncomfortable step in itself. Remember that "tell and listen" is just as important in your sexual relationships as in other relationships. Decide how and when you will speak with your partner, and practice what you want to say if you feel nervous. Also remember that sexual relationships, like other relationships, "ebb and flow." There will be times when the two of you are more sexually attracted to each other and times when this is less so. If your sexual attraction to each other wanes, it does not mean that your relationship is over; you can still be loving and caring towards each other.

Any relationship will benefit from you studying it more closely and analyzing the obstacles, as you have done before. You can use a similar approach in analyzing sex-related stresses. For example:

Feeling	Thought	Alternative
Numb: I'm drifting away.	That hurt! I can't stand this. This is dirty	I'm pulling away because what he just did reminded me of past abuse. It's not his fault and our love making isn't dirty . . . **Action: . . . but I'll have to explain what's just happened otherwise it can get worse**
Panic and hurt	I've done so much to please her, and she still wants more. I must be really inadequate	Perhaps she wants me to do more because she enjoys our sexual relationship. I know that I tend to feel inadequate

		very easily and it's not like her to do anything to upset me **Action: We need to talk about this. I'll ask her about it in the morning when I don't feel so vulnerable**
Furious	I'm washing up and he paws me. All men are the same: one thing on their mind. It's an insult	He hugged me. It was probably affectionate and I over-reacted because I'm sensitive to physical contact. He's actually a really sensitive man and very respectful **Action: I'll try to explain to him why I reacted so strongly**

Feelings About Ourselves and Our Bodies

In Part One of this book we explored some of the consequences of having been abused as a child, and we saw that having a poor self-image and even disliking one's body is quite common. This is bound to affect the way that one feels about physical relationships. In Chapter 12, you read about improving your self-image, and it is worth revisiting this chapter if a poor self-image interferes with your current physical relationship.

Your past experiences of abuse, particularly sexual abuse and teasing about your appearance, may have left you very confused and even negative in your feelings about your body. Some survivors are deeply ashamed of their bodies and go to great lengths to disguise their appearance or their sexuality. For example, some use baggy or dull clothing so as not to look sexually inviting, while others wear very sexy clothing because they feel asexual and try to achieve a sexual identity through their dress. Some make up carefully in order to compensate for feeling unattractive. Some use excess weight to hide their sexuality, while some diet continuously to try to achieve a sexually attractive body, and some women starve to get rid of the breasts and hips that remind them of their sexuality. One of the first steps in sexual recovery is developing more positive feelings about your body.

Exercise

- Try to imagine a child who has never been sexually abused or tormented about his or her body. What do you think helps that child develop a liking for its body?
- The things that help a child learn to feel comfortable about its body are the same things that can help you develop a better relationship with yours.
- These might include: dressing up and learning to take a pride in appearance; receiving compliments (this might be among your relationship ground rules); nudity not being sexualized; physical exercise and learning to enjoy one's body; discovering pleasant sensations: splashing in water, being wrapped in a soft towel, wearing silky clothes, etc.
- Make notes on what you could you do to help you to begin to like your body. For example: treating your body with oils and lotions; paying more attention to your appearance; feeding your body with healthy foods.
- Finally, be diligent in not comparing yourself *only* with the *most* attractive men or women; you are only setting yourself up to feel disappointed.

State of Mind and Sexual Relationships

Our state of mind very much influences our enjoyment of a sexual relationship. This term covers many topics: spacing out, our mood and the sexual myths that we believe.

Spacing Out

The only way that many children cope with abuse is by "spacing out." Some manage to tolerate the most terrible physical assaults because of an ability to detach from reality. This is such a powerful and effective coping response that survivors of abuse often carry it into adulthood. In the past, threat was the trigger that set off this response, and for the adult survivor, the intimacy or the physical nature of sex can feel like a threat. Even affectionate physical contact in a safe setting can sometimes trigger dissociation.

Try to catch, analyze and challenge your fears. You may be able to dispel some of them and you might find yourself spacing out less. If it helps your understanding of the process, revisit the section on "Spacing Out" in Chapter 2. Talk with your partner, explain what happens to you and why. The two of you might be able to change and to vary your love-making so that you are less likely to dissociate.

Finally, don't expect to be able to simply stop spacing out because you have put your mind to it: these protective responses tend only to fade over time as we become more confident.

Mood

All of us find that our current mood affects our sexual appetite: and depression, stress and illness, in particular, affect our mood. If you are stressed at home or work, if you are ill or recovering from illness, your sex drive will diminish. A woman's sexual appetite can also change over the course of the month and, if you are a pre-menopausal woman, you might consider monitoring this.

Anger towards a partner can have a very marked effect on libido. Don't expect to be able to achieve a satisfactory sexual relationship with someone towards whom you have unresolved feelings of anger. You will need to set aside time for dealing with this.

Myths about Sex

These are the "old wives' tales" about sex that are passed around, but have no foundation in reality. We are not going to challenge them here, just label them as myths. Some common myths are listed below: perhaps you can challenge them for yourself.

Myths about sex:
- All physical contact leads to sex

- Men always want sex and must be ready for sex: if not they are inadequate and/or their partner is unattractive
- To have sex, a man must have an erection
- To be sexy, we must be young and beautiful with a good body (Even if we aren't young, we have still have to have a perfect body)
- Nice girls don't have sex before marriage
- Good wives have lots of sex after marriage
- Women must have orgasms to enjoy sex
- Partners must orgasm together
- Good sex means swinging from the chandelier
- Sex is over when the man ejaculates
- Women never fake
- It's bad to get aroused and not have sex
- Saying "No" is unacceptable
- Homosexuality / bisexuality is wrong
- Being attracted to the same sex means I'm homosexual

If you discuss myths with a close friend, you'll probably come up with even more.

In bad sexual relationships, these and other myths about sex often get wheeled out to hurt and demean a partner. If you have already addressed the nonsense of the myths, you can better protect yourself against the hurt if this happens to you.

Painful Sex

Penetrative sex can be extremely painful for those who have been injured by sexual intercourse or who are frightened by the prospect of penetrative sex. Some pain might be the result of physical damage and, although it is often difficult to discuss this with a family doctor or a gynaecologist, you should have a physical examination if you think that physical damage lies behind your pain. Some physical conditions that cause pain are easily treated, such as pelvic infections in women or a tight foreskin in men.

This will mean talking about something very intimate and, possibly, having an internal examination, so you must choose your doctor carefully as you will need to be able to trust her or him.

Another explanation for painful sex is muscular tension. In women who have pain on vaginal intercourse, this is called vaginismus. It is caused by the muscles surrounding the vagina contracting so tightly that penetration is painful, if not impossible. Even when a woman is aroused, tensing can be a reflex action that then makes penetration difficult. Although lubricants can sometimes help, the key is learning to relax.

The approach used by sex therapists involves first helping a person learn how to relax (there are some guidelines for relaxing in Chapter 10). Then penetration is achieved gradually through a series of steps, some carried out by both partners and some carried out by the partner experiencing pain. Often this requires a course of therapy, but the stages are simplified and outlined below. Some of the self-help books at the end of this chapter carry more detailed descriptions of this procedure.

Individual Work   The woman who experiences pain first learns to relax and, in this state and using lubrication, gently introduces a finger into her vagina. If masturbation, at this time, makes the experience easier and more pleasurable, then this is a good thing. When she feels comfortable with one finger, she can introduce a second and perhaps a third finger. The goal is for the woman to be able to remain relaxed and to feel pleasure when she is penetrated vaginally.

Work as a Couple   Together, partners can gradually work towards achieving pleasurable penetration, but good communication and a caring sexual relationship is essential for this to be possible. In step one, partners avoid penetration and, instead, focus on giving each other pleasure without making genital contact. For some this is the first time that a close and sensual relationship has not been overtly sexual, and many find a new dimension of pleasure when they learn how to please each other in a physical, but non-sexual way.

When both partners feel comfortable with this level of physical contact, they can move on to step two and begin to touch each other in a sexual way, but without penetration. Again, partners learn how to have a relaxing and gratifying sexual relationship without having to have penetrative sex.

Both step one and step two encourage partners to be more creative and to engage in foreplay. Foreplay is a crucial part of a relaxed sexual relationship and a necessary prelude to step three.

In step three, when *both* partners feel ready and relaxed, they can attempt penetrative intercourse. Again, this needs to be gentle and gradual, so that pain is avoided.

Finally, it is useful to recognize that penetration can take place in a number of positions, some more comfortable than others. Often, experimenting with different positions can ease discomfort.

Sex in the Future

From now on, you need to prioritize and express your own needs regarding sex. This can be frightening. You may fear losing your partner; you may fear the feelings of sexual arousal; you may fear that you will "fail" sexually. But, in order to learn to enjoy your sexuality, you need to rebuild from a safe sexual foundation.

Each person's starting point will be different. Some will start by learning to get sensual pleasure from the body, for example by using body lotions and oils. Others will be able to begin by developing ways of giving themselves sexual pleasure through reading or watching erotic material and through masturbation. A person can learn to heighten physical pleasure with or without a partner.

Those with a partner can involve that person in confidence-building through hand-holding, cuddling and other non-threatening activities. You do need to define what activities are not threatening to you and set your boundaries there. If you need to say "No" to sex, say "No" to sex. If you don't set limits, you will never feel safe enough to begin exploring your sexuality.

Over time, as your sexual confidence increases, you will be able to engage in increasingly sexual activities. However, allow yourself to go at your own pace.

Useful Contacts and Further Reading

Those couples who need extra support in improving their sexual relationship can contact their local "Relate" counselling service for further guidance.

You might also find the following books helpful:

The Mirror Within, by A. Dickson (Quartet Books, 1985)
The Relate Guide to Sex in Loving Relationships, by S. Litvinoff (Vermilion, 1992)
Incest and Sexuality, by W. Maltz and B. Holman (Lexington Books, 1987)
Sexual Happiness for Men, by M. Yaffe and E. Fenwick (Dorling Kindersley, 1986)
Sexual Happiness for Women, by M. Yaffe and E. Fenwick (Dorling Kindersley, 1986)
Men and Sex, by B. Zilbergeld (Bantam Books, 1999; HarperCollins, 1993)

20

Reflecting On Losses

Children who had to grow up too soon, or who had to keep shameful family secrets, or who learnt to dislike themselves so much that they didn't have friends, lost important parts of their childhood. They didn't experience the full freedom and carelessness of childhood, or the security of childhood that provides a safe base for learning, exploring and growing into a confident adult. Children whose parents abused them lost out on good parenting: they didn't have the trusting, safe relationship with a parent that helps a child learn social confidence and self-reliance.

As you review your past experiences, you may find yourself reflecting on things that you have lost or missed out on, and you may find yourself feeling deeply saddened by this. Such feelings are perfectly normal – grieving is often part of the recovery process. You may continue grieving for some time, particularly if you gradually recall more and more that you have lost.

The Process of Grieving

Grieving is often painful, as it means accepting that your wish that things were different may never be realized. You may feel more depressed or agitated for a while, and therefore need more support from others when you go through this phase of recovery. Again, use your coping skills and try to nurture yourself through this stage. Self-nurturing is especially important during grieving.

Your losses are going to reflect both those from the past and those in the present. There may be aspects of childhood which you were denied because of your abusive experiences. For example, you may have been deprived of a sense of trust and security, a sense of self-worth and the feeling that you were like other kids. Some of your losses will relate to the present. You may need to say "goodbye" to people who never really existed for you and grieve over that loss – for example, the loss of the *good* mother, the *protective* father, the *loving* sister that you never had and will never have. Sometimes, key relationships can improve over time, but you may find that you have to let go of hopes that these people will ever exist for you.

You might have hoped that, one day, you would understand why you were abused or unprotected; but key people might be dead or refuse to communicate with you, in which case you will have to let go of the hope that you'll get an explanation, an answer to the question "Why?" At some point you have to accept that you will never really know and you will have to stop searching.

Exercise

- Spend some time thinking about and listing both what you lost in the past and what you will have to let go of now.
- If you have not done this before, you might only now begin the process of grieving.

Grieving is more than a feeling of sadness. Indeed, it's not just one feeling, but a whole succession of emotions which might overlap and which can take a while to work through. There is often a time of *feeling numb*; then a time of *yearning* for what is lost, which might turn into a *preoccupation* which gets in the way of doing other things. Some people get very *angry* when they consider their losses; another common feeling is *guilt*, either because of this anger or because they feel that they were responsible for the loss.

You can better appreciate and work through the stage that you find yourself in if you analyze what's happening and why.

Once again, you can use the familiar format of catching your feelings and thoughts and then using this as a basis for under-standing what's going on and, where possible, what is the best next step for you.

Feelings	Thoughts	Explanation and action
Tense, stressed	I can't stop going over things in my mind: am I going to lose control?	This is part of what I have to do to work through the past. If I ignore the hurt, I can't grieve and put it behind me **Action: I'll give myself more time and I'll not worry about reflecting on the past so much. If I feel I'm getting ob-sessed, I'll go and talk with my doctor**
Angry, furious	We could have had a normal relationship, a good relationship, if she hadn't always put each new boyfriend first	It's no wonder that I'm angry. All the misery I went through was avoidable and our relationship was wasted **Action: I'm going to write down my feelings in a letter. I don't know if I'll send it or not**
Guilty	I should have done more to help myself. I threw away chances	I was a junior school kid, terrified of everyone and everything. I did well just to keep my head above water **Action: I'm not going to be so hard on myself. I'll get out the old photographs to remind me just how young I was**

As time passes, the fierce pain will fade, but you might always have a sense of loss – this is quite natural. It is preferable to move forward, accepting this sense of loss, than to remain "stuck" with unrealistic hope. Don't stay in the past, but try to deal with it and move on.

Crying

As a child, you might have learnt not to cry, and perhaps you haven't been able to cry as an adult. Many of us learn rules about crying such as "Crying is weak," or we form our own beliefs about tearfulness, like:

If I start, I'll never be able to stop
If I start crying, I'll lose all control over my emotions
Crying makes me vulnerable
If I don't cry, I don't feel pain

Some of these beliefs were true when you were a child. An abused child might discover that crying makes the abuser more cruel, or that emotionally detaching did deaden the pain for a while, for example. In adulthood, however, these beliefs stop us from expressing sadness and hurt in a very natural way.

Exercise

- Set aside time to explore your beliefs about crying, and ask yourself whether or not they are true for you as an adult.
- Ask yourself if you carry beliefs about crying that are actually getting in the way of your recovery.

You can't force tears, so let crying happen naturally. If you find that you are beginning to cry as an adult, don't be afraid or contemptuous of tears. Remember that:

- crying is the most natural response to sadness and loss;
- generally, it is better to cry than to bottle up the feelings;
- bottled-up grief forms a "reservoir," so when you do start to cry, you'll find that there are more tears than you expected; this can *feel* overwhelming, but you will keep control.

Replacing Losses

Although you might have to accept significant losses or the lack of good parenting in your childhood, you can strive to replace some of these deficits in your life.

For example, think about your childhood. What important experiences were missing? A greater sense of security? Some times of real peace? More "playtimes," just for enjoyment? More friends and openness? We can never rewrite the past, but you could start compensating for missing out when you were young by working on your social life so that you gain more of a sense of security, and you could make time for yourself which is quality, peaceful time or time for fun.

If you were denied good parenting, what was missing? Perhaps you needed to be told that you were special and made to feel safe, or to be spoken to gently and reassured when you were frightened. Perhaps you needed to feel accepted and "good enough." Again, you can take steps towards parenting yourself, nurturing yourself, building your own sense of being special and giving yourself the comfort that you did not have as a child.

Exercise

- Set aside some time for thinking this through, noting what losses you can now compensate for, and the ways in which you can do this.
- Ask: "What was missing from my childhood?" and then try to balance this with: "How I can make up for this now."

Putting the Past in Its Place

This is what you are moving towards. As you recover, you will eventually reach the stage of resolving problems and moving on. In time, you may find that your experience of abuse becomes a memory which will come to mind, but which is no longer predominant in your life. It will always remain part of your history, but you can move on. Putting the past in its place will free you up to concentrate on your future.

Further Reading

When you are working on this part of your recovery, you might find it helpful to read the following books:

Overcoming Depression, by Paul Gilbert (Robinson, 1997; revised edition 2000)
A *Safer Place to Cry,* by B. Roet (Optima, 1989)

21

Looking After Yourself From Now On

Living With Setbacks

You will almost certainly find that recovery is a process of ups and downs, that setbacks will occur and that they will be disappointing. Even though a setback can be distressing, it is not "a failure" or "the beginning of the end" – a setback is a lapse from which you can learn more about your needs and vulnerabilities. In fact, the key to living with setbacks is reviewing them and asking: "What have I learnt?"

Again, a setback isn't "all or nothing." There is a spectrum of responses ranging from coping with little difficulty, through struggling to cope, lapsing and, ultimately, having a major setback or relapse.

❏ .... ❏
Coping with little   Struggle   Lapse   Major setback:
difficulty   relapse

Even a major setback, or relapse, does not mark the end of your progress. We can all recover and learn from any setback. In fact, setbacks contribute to progress because each offers us the chance to understand more about our needs. Then we can take steps to protect ourselves in the future. Once you have analyzed a setback, you can plan, with hindsight, how you will tackle similar situations in the future, and this will lessen your vulnerability. When you do experience a lapse, use your skills in challenging the negative automatic thoughts that come to mind.

196

I'd stuck to a healthy eating plan for five weeks and I began to introduce some treats so that I didn't get bored with my diet. So far so good. As you know, I love chocolate and so I bought several of my favorite brands. What a mistake! I fell straight back into my old cycle of overeating, then feeling bad and then comfort eating again. So what have I learned? I still think that it's a good idea to make my diet more interesting, but it's too soon to for me to buy tempting food in quantity. So, I'll only buy a small amount of chocolate each day and I'll try to vary my diet with less irresistible foods.

My mood had been quite good for a couple of months and I felt more like my old self. I got less careful about taking my antidepressants regularly, but I felt OK at first. Then I started to recognize the depression coming back again. I stopped going out and just sat at home being really scared that I was losing it again, and things got worse quite quickly. Fortunately, I had to visit the doctor about something else and she immediately put me back on the full dose of antidepressants. Looking back, it seems like a silly thing for me to have done because I knew that it's best to take the medicine for several months. It was a hard lesson to learn, but next time, I'm taking no chances: if I start to feel low, I'm going to see my doctor quickly instead of becoming a recluse again.

I hadn't harmed myself for months and I was feeling confident that I could resist the urges. I suppose I'd reached a stage where I wanted to test myself. I bought tablets and razor blades because I wanted to prove that I could resist – and I did, but only for two days. I wasn't to know that things at work would become very difficult and that my boyfriend and I would have a huge row. But these things did happen, I became really upset and the urges were too strong to resist. I had the pills and blades so I used them. I felt so bad afterwards. I felt as though I'd let myself down and all those who'd been helpful and supportive to me, but I was determined not to get into a rut so I made some decisions. I'm not going to "test" myself again because it's too risky to have tablets and razor blades in the house if I feel fragile, and next time I'm upset, I'll turn to friends first.

Some setbacks might be predictable, and if you can foresee risk situations, you can devise your management strategy straight away. The beauty of having a well-prepared management strategy is that you don't have to come up with a solution in a time of crisis because you've already done so (see Table 21.1 for three examples). However, you do need to have your plan readily available, so keep it where you can find it quickly: on a filing card in a wallet, or on a page in your personal organizer, for example.

There are blank copies of this management strategy in the appendix.

Table 21.1:	**Management Strategy**		
1. Risk situation	*2. Thought*	*3. Alternative*	*4. Action*
PMT	I must binge: I am weak	This week has been unusually stressful, so I'm feeling more vulnerable. I can expect this and I have coped in the past	Get support: phone Suzy. Go swimming for distraction. Eat a banana to take the edge off the craving
Pam leaves me	I am not lovable and never will be	Pam said that she did love me, but that she had her own problems to work on	Visit friends for support and distraction. Work on my social life, rather than withdrawing
Visit the family	It was my fault that I was abused	I was abused because he made that choice: it was not my fault	Leave as soon as possible. Avoid future visits until I feel stronger

5. Worst outcome	6. Thoughts	7. Alternative	8. Action
Binge for days. Gain 8lb.	I'm disgusting: I'll never take control of my eating pattern	Even when I hit a really difficult patch, it doesn't last forever. I do get back on track and the weight goes again	It's best if I try to relax, rather than stay uptight about this. I'll go back to planning my meals carefully until I feel back in control
Depression	It's true that I'm not lovable and I'll always be miserable. It's not worth trying	No wonder I feel down, I've lost an important, close friend. This isn't about my being lovable or not	I'm going to make sure to keep up my other social contacts and I'll write to Pam to let her know that I'm still here for her if she needs me
Depression and cutting myself	I'm weird: I'm bad: I'll never change	I'm normal, I'm simply having a setback, just like I predicted. I've learnt that I'm not ready to spend time in the family home, yet. The way things are going, I will change and I will get stronger	I'll write home so that I can keep in touch with Mum and the boys, but won't visit. At this time, I'll concentrate on being with the friends that make me feel safe and cared for

Columns 1 and 2 will be familiar, as you will now be used to recognizing when you cope less well and the thoughts that you get at such times. You are probably getting used to coming up with balanced, alternative ways of appraising things along with an action plan to take you forward (columns 3 and 4). In order to devise a full management strategy, you now need to take this further, first by considering the worst possible outcome (column 5) and the type of thoughts that you would have at that time (column 6). Then, you need to stand back and come up with a more balanced alternative to even your worst thoughts (column 7) and, as usual, follow this by planning what you could do to make sure that you did not stay in a rut (column 8). This will sound like a great deal of work – and it is; but remember that these plans are your protection against relapse.

Of course, it is possible that you will have a relapse from time to time – in fact, it's almost inevitable. The best thing you can do, if this happens, is ask yourself:

- "What have I learnt from this?"
- "What will I do differently in the future?"

By answering these questions, you will have developed valuable insights into your needs and vulnerabilities, which you can use in subsequent planning.

Exercise

- Use the format in Table 21.1 to help you make a record of your risk situations and coping plan.
- You are probably familiar with your "high risk" situations for distress, so take some time to brainstorm and write them down (column 1). Once you have identified risky situations, try to predict your typical negative thoughts (column 2). Use this as the basis for planning how you would challenge them and come up with an alternative way of viewing the situation (column 3). Then, consider what action you could take, what you could do to feel better (column 4).
- Setbacks mark a time of vulnerability, so prepare for the worst (columns 5–8) and then be pleased if it doesn't come to this.
- Even though it might sometimes be difficult, consider

continued on next page

---

the worst outcome of the setback (column 5): you might lapse into overeating, spending or drinking, for example. Predict your negative thoughts if this did happen (column 6) and, again, challenge them (column 7) and think how you can take things forward (column 8). In this way, you are developing a thorough relapse prevention plan.
- Keep a record of your risk situations and coping plan, as you will find it difficult to recall it when you are distressed. Anticipate adding to this and modifying this plan over time.

Devising an Effective Action Plan

Your action plan is often your main coping strategy in a crisis. If it is going to stave off relapse, it has to be a realistic substitute for your problem behavior or problem thoughts. That is, the action that you take has to "match" your needs at the time. In the first example in Table 21.1, the problem was a craving to overeat, and the solution that best matched the need in this person was eating a banana in order to take the edge off the craving in a safe, satisfying way. The second person was at risk of worsening depressive thoughts, and used rational self-talk and distraction specifically to combat the thoughts; the third person was at risk as long as he stayed in the family home, and his action was to leave. Each of the strategies matches the risk situation.

There are more examples in Table 21.2. In these cases, you will see that two people, on the face of it, share the same problem. However, what makes sense of the problem differs in each case. So, their problem reactions serve different functions, or have different meanings. This means that the action plan for coping will need to be different for each of the people who share the same problem.

Table 21.2: Understanding What's Behind a Problem Reaction

Problem reaction	What makes sense of this (Person 1)	What makes sense of this (Person 2)
Anxiety in the street	I'm afraid that I'll pass out	I'm afraid others are looking at me and thinking badly of me
Overeating	I just want to put things out of my mind and this helps	I feel nervous and this calms me
Spiralling down in mood	Being negative feels familiar and I'm good at it. It's the easy option	I'm alone and all I can think about is how bleak and hopeless things are
Drinking too much	It makes me feel sociable and less of a misfit if I join in	It helps me drown out my sorrows
Self-injury	I don't feel so numb and dead inside when I hurt myself: it reminds me I'm alive	Hurting myself distracts me from the real deep-down pain
Attempting suicide	I want some peace: I'll take the risk	I don't care if I live or die: I'll leave it to fate

Once a person has made sense of the problem reaction it is possible to think what might be a reasonable substitute, for example:

Anxiety in the street   In this case, both would need to be able to challenge their negative thought, but Person 1 will benefit from developing arguments against passing out in the street, such as: *"I've done this before without fainting. Worrying makes me light-headed and so I'll try to calm myself. I won't overdo things: I'll take on a little more each day until I regain my confidence."*

On the other hand, Person 2 needs to develop an argument to restore self-confidence, like: *"I can't mind read so I don't know what others are thinking of me. Just because I feel something, it isn't fact: I feel as though I'm being looked at but this probably isn't so. If I relax a little, I'll feel less self conscious."*

Overeating   Here, Person 1 would benefit from finding something else as a distraction from troublesome thoughts, rather than eating: phoning a friend, for example, or exercising, or computer games.

Person 2, however, is unlikely to find this helpful and for this individual a better strategy would be finding a relaxing alternative to eating: yoga, relaxation exercises or taking a soothing bath, for example.

Spiralling down in mood   Person 1 is very vulnerable because her familiar, negative thoughts are so prominent. She needs to have prepared a verbal challenge to these thoughts; if she hasn't, she needs to distract herself from them, perhaps using some of the ideas in Chapter 11.

Person 2, however, ruminates because of his social isolation, so he needs to have a plan to help him contact friends or talk with someone. If friends aren't available, he could use a helpline; but when he is feeling stronger, he should begin working on his social life, so that he isn't so lonely and vulnerable in the future.

Drinking too much   Person 1, in this example, is striving to fit in with the crowd and feel sociable. He could still mix with his friends but substitute non-alcoholic drinks or low-alcohol beers or wines.

Person 2, in contrast, is hoping to achieve distraction from her misery. There are other ways to achieve this, for example, contacting someone who can support her, whether this is a friend or a profesional or a person from a non-statutory organization like The Samaritans.

Self-injury   Here, Person 1 is seeking confirmation that he can feel alive instead of numb, so could try alternative behaviors like exciting or vigorous exercise. This wouldn't help Person 2, who is seeking distraction from inner pain. In this instance a more appropriate substitute might be self-nurturing or safe distraction techniques like using soothing mental images (see Chapter 11).

Another common reason for self-injury is the feeling that one should be hurt or punished. If you experience this and find it very compelling, then try to think of some less harmful ways of hurting or punishing yourself. For example, strenuous exercise can be painful without causing damage, holding ice cubes in the mouth or taking cold showers can be painful without causing injury. Alternatively, volunteering to do unpleasant tasks, like emptying rubbish bins or doing very repetitive jobs that no one else likes, can substitute for self-punishment. Ideally, as your self-esteem grows you will not feel the need to hurt or to punish yourself, so these are only interim tactics.

Attempting suicide   In this case, there is no doubt that **it would be best if both sought professional help**, although each attempts suicide for different reasons. Person 1 is seeking some peace, from stress and pain. She doesn't necessarily want to die, but she's reached a point where it's worth the risk, if she escapes the torment for a while. For her there might be other ways of achieving some respite: some meditations and grounding exercises (see Chapter 11) can offer temporary respite. Sometimes this is sufficient to get through the bleakest period.

Person 2 is at a different stage: he's become ambivalent about living or dying. Therefore, he could refer to a self-harm prevention plan to remind himself of all the reasons he has for living (see Chapter 12). This might then curb the urgency to kill himself.

These alternative reactions aim to take the edge off the urge to resort to old, unhelpful responses. It is only fair to recognize that the balanced thoughts or the safe behaviors that you use are often only pale substitutes for the usual responses. They are rarely as compelling as the familiar reactions and are usually not so immediately powerful. Don't be disappointed if you don't get the usual quick relief, or high, or comfort from your alternative reaction, and don't be surprised if it's hard to put it into action – after all, you are practiced at the old response, so it's bound to come more easily.

Exercise

- Make sure that your action plans are realistic, first by exploring what the problem response means to you, what makes sense of it, why it happens.
- Then you can brainstorm "matching" solutions.
- If you have friends who can help you with this, all the better as friends are often creative in problem solving.

By learning to live with setbacks and getting into the habit of learning from them while curbing the unhelpful responses to upsets, you will be better able to look after yourself from now on. This doesn't come naturally, so anticipate having to work at it.

22

Continuing the Work

Preparing for the Future

You are coming to the end of this book, but this does not necessarily mean that you have completed the healing process: your progress will continue for some time yet. You might be ready to put certain issues behind you, but you may want to revisit certain topics.

You have probably made significant changes in your life and might be feeling stronger and more at ease than you used to, but you will need to keep practicing your new skills and putting into action your new resolutions. This will keep you on the path of recovery.

Now you have identified your losses, and grieved for them, you may want to think about your hopes and wishes for the future. What are your new ambitions? What are your goals for future relationships? What steps would you need to take to ensure that future relationships are not damaging to you and that your ambitions are realized?

It is worth thoroughly considering what you need to do in order to keep moving on. Rather than simply holding ideas in mind, make notes for yourself and make a commitment to keep working at your recovery. The more concrete your commitment, the more likely you are to continue the work of recovery.

Don't forget your relapse management plan from Chapter 21. Recovery will involve successes and failures, and you will benefit from anticipating these times and having your coping plan ready. In this way you can minimize the likelihood of a lapse turning into a more serious relapse. You can also reduce the probability of relapse by organizing your life around your needs. For example, if you have had a drinking problem, avoid having alcohol readily available; if you know that loneliness triggers depression, commit yourself to social events; and so on. This is all part of your ongoing recovery.

Increasing Self-Reliance

If you were abused as a child, you might well have grown up lacking confidence in your ability to take charge and look after yourself. This might have been the case when you were small, but you've done a great deal of developing since then and you can begin to become more reliant on yourself, to trust in yourself more. So you can anticipate increasing your self-reliance; but remember that it takes time and involves setbacks. You might find it helpful to start keeping a journal of your progress and your achievements so that you have something to refer to if you do get despondent.

Sometimes becoming more self-reliant can seem frightening, and there's the temptation to slip back and relinquish control. On the other hand, some find themselves going a bit "over the top" when they first try to take control of their life. Try to find a balance whereby you keep moving forward without pushing others out of the way. If it is a struggle to keep a balance, try to understand why this is. Do you have unhelpful beliefs about taking control, for example? These might be something like:

If I start to take control, others won't like me
If I take control, no one will see that I still need support
If I don't take absolute control, others will take advantage of me
If I don't have complete control, I'll lose control

If you can identify what drives an unhelpful reaction, you can begin to modify it. Get into the habit of asking yourself "Why?" whenever you find yourself struggling with something. When a problem seems particularly thorny, try returning to the six questions that you learnt in Chapter 13, using Diary 2 if necessary. This will help you make a thorough appraisal of a situation.

Moving Forward

When many clients come to our clinic, they refer to themselves as "victims." Many have indeed spent a great deal of their lives as "victims" and it isn't surprising that's the feeling they have. When they begin the process of recovery, however long it takes, it's fair to say they are "survivors." As "survivors" of abuse learn to deal with the trauma that they've been through and begin to put it in the past, most find that they want to leave behind the labels and refer to themselves, not as ex-"victims" and not as "survivors," but as regular persons with their own identity. You might find that you feel the same way; after all, there is much more to you than your traumatic history.

Recovery can take months or years, and some say that they feel it's a lifelong process. Remember that, simply by reading this book, you will have moved forward, and you can never return to "square one" – you have learnt too much. If you feel dispirited and need a reminder that things can change, read "Lucy's" account of recovery in the Epilogue.

Useful Contacts and Further Reading

Also bear in mind that you don't have to continue your recovery alone, if it is too difficult. There are professional counsellors and therapists available, and there are organizations that are willing to help. There are also other books which can help you to recover and increase your self-reliance. Below are a few which others have found helpful.

For survivors of abuse:

Breaking Free, by C. Ainscough and K. Toon (Sheldon, 1993; 2000)
Out in the Open, by Q. Bain and M. Sanders (Virago Upstarts, 1990)
Toxic Parents, by S. Forward (Bantam Books, 1990)
Outgrowing the Pain, by E. Gil (Dell Books, 1983)
Victims No Longer, by M.Lew (Perennial Library, 1990)

For specific problems:

Overcoming Social Anxiety and Shyness, by Gillian Butler
(Robinson/New York University Press, 1999)

Bulimia Nervosa And Binge-Eating, by Peter Cooper (Robinson/
New York University Press, 1993)

Overcoming Low Self-Esteem by Melanie Fennell (Robinson/
New York University Press, 1999)

Overcoming Depression, by Paul Gilbert (Robinson, 1997;
revised edition 2000)

Overcoming Anxiety, by Helen Kennerley (Robinson/New York
University Press, 1997)

General cognitive therapy texts:

Manage Your Mind (US: *Managing Your Mind*), by G. Butler
and T. Hope (Oxford University Press, 1996)

Mind Over Mood, by D. Greenberger and C. Padesky (Guilford,
1995)

Re-Inventing Your Life, by J. Young and J. Klosko (Plume, 1994)

There are a number of groups and organizations which can help
you continue with your recovery. Local contact numbers will
be in your phone book under 'Counseling' or 'Counselling'.

If you've got this far, then you should congratulate yourself on
working through this book. I hope that you will have learnt helpful ways of understanding and dealing with a range of difficulties and I would encourage you to keep your recovery high on
your agenda.

Epilogue

For several years, "Lucy" battled to overcome the memories and legacies of her traumatic past. It wasn't easy, but she got there; and she has written this epilogue as an encouragement to others.

People said they believed in me but I didn't believe them as I didn't believe in me – but I do now.

Upon achieving recovery, many clichés spring to mind like: "sunshine after rain" and "dreams can come true." I thought that these would never hold real meaning for me – but now they do.

It's incredibly difficult to put into words how I feel now, as it's so different from the infinite blackness, hellish despair and painful voids that filled my mind for years. I was so used to bad thoughts and feelings occupying every waking and sleeping moment that to concentrate on the good ones originally felt alien to me.

Now, after persevering through the seemingly endless nightmare, the sense of happiness, completeness and satisfaction in achieving my goal of life and belief in myself is great!

It was beyond my grasp and out of my reach that I'd make it – but a deep inner determined strength fought on and on and on – and won!

I didn't wake up one morning and everything felt OK and hunky dory – it was more of a gradual realization that the positives were very slowly overcoming the negatives until this turned into a permanent state of mind.

Epilogue

Instead of just existing – I'm now living! I'm no longer a shell, but alive; and it's fantastic!!!

Index

Appendix

In this section, you will find copies of the diaries and recording sheets which have been described in the book. Generally speaking, people find that self-monitoring, or using recording sheets like the ones in the appendix, contributes to a quicker recovery, so I would encourage you to use these sheets.

If you find that the format of some doesn't quite suit you, try to modify it so that is of more use to you. It is not crucially important to fill in the printed sheets perfectly, but it is important that you collect information that is helpful to you: that's the whole point of self-monitoring.

If you think that you will need more copies, simply photocopy a set of the sheets before you fill them in.

Diary 1

Monitor your feelings each day, noting when you feel upset or particularly good. Jot down what was happening at the time. Then, see if you can catch what was going through your mind and note what you did. Note these details as near to the time of the distress as you can – it is easy to forget later!

Date/time	EMOTIONS How I felt	ENVIRONMENT What was happening at the time	THOUGHTS OR IMAGES What was going through my mind	BEHAVIOR What I did

Recording Sheet: The Way I Cope

Try to monitor your levels of distress each day, noting when you feel particularly upset. Jot down what set off the distress and, so that you can judge change, give yourself a rating for how bad it feels. Use the simple scale, below, to rate your distress. Note what you did in response to the feeling upset. Then, in order to see how well your coping strategy worked, re-rate your distress levels.

1	2	3	4	5	6	7	8	9	10
No distress, calm				Moderate distress				As distressed as possible	

Record all those occasions when your rating is 6 or more. Note these details as near to the time of the distress as you can – it is easy to forget later!

Date/time	Rating	What was happening at the time?	What I did in response to the feelings	Re-rating

Diary 2: Analysing Biased Thinking

Monitor your feelings each day, noting when you feel particularly upset or particularly good. Jot down what went through your mind at the time. When you feel distressed, try to identify thinking biases and then see if you can challenge the upsetting thought. When you have worked out a challenging statement, re-rate your distress so that you can see the impact of your challenge. Rate your distress on the following scale:

1	2	3	4	5	6	7	8	9	10
No distress, calm				Moderate distress				As distressed as possible	

Note these details as near to the time of the distress as you can – it is easy to forget later!

Date/time	What was going through my mind?	Distress rating	What were my thinking biases?	How would I view the situation now?	Re-rating

'Positive' Record

Date	Good things about me

WEEKLY SUMMING UP:

My Management Strategy

1. Risk situation	2. Thoughts	3. Alternative	4. Action

5. WORST OUTCOME	6. THOUGHTS	7. ALTERNATIVE	8. ACTION